THE TRUTH SHALL SET YOU FREE:

GLOBAL ANGLICANS IN THE 21ST CENTURY

EDITED BY CHARLES RAVEN

The Latimer Trust

CONTENTS

Foreword

The Most Revd Dr Peter Jensen

The Global Fellowship of Confessing Anglicans is a theological and spiritual movement within the heart of the Anglican Communion. It began as a practical response to a major crisis within the Communion. But because it is grounded in a vital biblical theology expressed in the Jerusalem Declaration and Statement it has transcended its origins and offers fellowship and spiritual renewal to Anglicans throughout the world.

The GFCA has a twofold aim.

First it exists to recognise and authenticate Anglican Christians who as a matter of profound theological conviction have been disaffiliated from their dioceses or denominations. In this way it has, for example, sustained the ecclesial life of many thousands of Anglican Christians in the USA and Canada who have had to withdraw from their original affiliations over matters touching on salvation itself.

Second it exists to stimulate renewal in the churches of the Anglican Communion as they proclaim and defend the gospel of Jesus Christ. We are aware that the presenting issue of the crisis, human sexuality, was at depth a contest over the authority of scripture and we wish to affirm that authority as opposed to the wisdom of this world.

Most of the essays in the present volume arose from the Leaders Conference held in London in April 3013. Taken together, they constitute a significant contribution to the ministry of the gospel in and through the Anglican churches. They address fundamental issues in a vital way and hence serve the needs of the Communion and of the GFCA.

I warmly commend them to you.

Peter Jensen

(General Secretary, GFCA)

Introduction

Revd Charles Raven

Jesus' words 'The Truth Shall Set You Free' (John 8:32) are the motto text of the Canterbury Compass Rose, a design set in the floor of the nave of Canterbury Cathedral in 1988 and subsequently adopted as the symbol of the Anglican Communion. It is a profound statement and yet in contemporary Anglicanism open to quite differing interpretations – to what truth exactly does this compass point – revealed truth, truth as the fruit of autonomous human reason or truth as 'authentic' living (whatever that might be)?[1]

The irony of the Compass Rose is that the Communion it denotes is increasingly without direction and has no agreement of substance about the truth it holds to. It was in response to this confusion that the first Global Anglican Future Conference was convened in 2008 and delegates affirmed in the closing paragraph of the Jerusalem Statement and Declaration that 'The primary reason we have come to Jerusalem and issued this declaration is to free our churches to give clear and certain witness to Jesus Christ'. The freedom they sought was the freedom which flows from receiving Jesus' word, a goal which becomes entirely clear when we read the Compass Rose motto in its context. Jesus says 'If you abide in my word, you are my disciples indeed. And you shall know the truth, and the truth shall make you free." (John 8:31,32).

Just as the Compass Rose can be recovered as a powerful symbol of revealed truth once the magnetic north of Scripture is restored, so GAFCON and its Global Fellowship of Confessing Anglicans seeks, under God and as a movement of the Spirit, not to depart from the Anglican Communion, but to make a major course correction for the twenty-first century by recovering our Anglican heritage of biblical and gospel centred ecclesiology.

So this compilation is offered as a resource for delegates to the second Global Anglican Future Conference of 2013 and for all who long

---

[1]   The description of the symbol by the Anglican Communion's Compass Rose Society does not give the reference for the text or even mention that the words are taken from the Bible.
http://www.compassrosesociety.org/category/CRS_Symbol/index.shtml

to see the Anglican Communion emerge from its present crisis with a new confidence in the inspired Scriptures and the mission of God to which they bear witness. Apart from the contributions of Stephen Noll and Colin Reed, this material originated in addresses and seminars given at the Fellowship of Confessing Anglicans Leaders' Conference held in London at St Mark's Battersea Rise in London in April 2012. Here is a sample of what the GAFCON movement has already achieved – creative thinking by leaders, pastors and theologians with a passion for the gospel and an infectious confidence for the future of a biblically faithful Anglican witness. Publication is not necessarily an endorsement of the particular views of each writer, but this collection of addresses and essays is offered in the hope that it will strengthen and stimulate our common Confessing Anglican mind as we gather in Nairobi to commit ourselves afresh to the Great Commission to make disciples of all nations.

It is very appropriate that right at the beginning of this volume is the Jerusalem Statement and Declaration generated at the birth of the GAFCON movement in 2008. The importance of this contemporary confession of Reformed Anglican faith is difficult to overstate. In the same year that the Lambeth Conference of bishops for the first time in its history actively avoided giving doctrinal and ethical guidance to the Communion, the GAFCON delegates in Jerusalem, including over 200 bishops, produced an incisive analysis of the spiritual bankruptcy of the Western dominated governance structures of the Communion and provided the global Communion with a statement of faithful teaching to meet the challenges of the twenty-first century.

The primary purpose of the Church in the twenty first century remains however the same as it has throughout all preceding centuries, the fulfilment of the Great Commission. Most Anglicans will agree on the importance of mission, but its meaning in contemporary Anglicanism is confused. It is routinely invoked in an appeal for institutional unity, but without any clarity as to what we actually mean by mission. Vague and diluted ideas of mission all too easily dissolve into general humanitarianism or the secular enthusiasm for lifestyle choices as rights. So it is vital that we are clear about the gospel which must be at the heart of truly biblical mission and unity. The conviction which runs through what follows is that it is the gospel through which the Church is called into being, it is the proclamation of the gospel which is the Church's mission and highest priority, and the gospel is the criterion by which the Church must shape its life. So it is of the utmost importance that we are clear about what that gospel is and at this point is included a brief but Scripturally rich statement of the gospel which repays careful reading and reflection.

Archbishop Eliud Wabukala's keynote address from the 2012 Leader's Conference sets the scene since 2008 and highlights key themes. He identifies the heart of the Anglican Communion crisis as spiritual, not something that can be solved merely by giving existing institutions a makeover. He sets out the priority of the movement as mission first and foremost, which entails the need to act to preserve the integrity of the faith entrusted to us. 'We defend the gospel' said the Archbishop 'because we want to promote the gospel'. There is a strong awareness in this address that although we have to contend for the gospel, we do so as those who are new creatures in Christ and submit to Christ as Lord, without arrogance and belligerence.

This theme is echoed in the Bible Reading from Colossians by John Yates III in which he sets out the radical transformation of character and relationships which should flow from our new life as members of the body of Christ. In a world where people are so prone to insecurity and anxiety, and therefore vulnerable to false teaching, we must 'lead God's people out of the shadows of religion and into the substance of Christ himself'.

Dr Mike Ovey, Principal of Oak Hill College London, opens up a compelling vision of the uniqueness of Jesus in revelation, creation and salvation in his treatment of Hebrews 1:1-4. He identifies the heart of the spiritual crisis as turning away from Christ as Lord and turning in upon ourselves. The troubles of the Anglican Communion flow from a rejection of the uniqueness and sufficiency of the Lord Jesus Christ as the one who is heir and therefore owner of all things. This opens the door to the blatant rejection of biblical teaching and morality which has triggered our current crisis, but human pride can be manifested in more subtle ways and he challenges both Western and non-Western forms of syncretism which can infiltrate even the thinking of those who identify themselves as orthodox.

Bishop Michael Nazir Ali's address then takes up the question of how God's people in the world organise their life together in a way which is shaped by the Lordship of Christ and therefore by the gospel. Christ is the head of his church and no human authority can usurp that role. In the Anglican Communion at the moment that usurpation comes not only actively through false teaching, but also passively through the failure to uphold biblical teaching. Such a situation requires that we act and 'we do not to wait forever for non-existent Instruments of decision-making to make decisions that they will never make.'

The GAFCON movement has however been very clear right from the outset that taking action does not mean leaving the Anglican Communion, and the Revd Dr Ashley Null takes us back to the theological principles of the English Reformers of the sixteenth Century who did not see themselves as a via media between Rome and Geneva, but simply as those who were true Catholics in contrast to the grave errors of what became known as Roman Catholicism. Their reformed principle of 'sola scriptura' governed the English Reformers' ecclesiology so that the whole of the church's life was shaped by the need to proclaim the gospel, but this did not mean sitting light to the past. It was, for instance, part of Cranmer's hermeneutical method to study extensively the Patristic writers, not because they were an equal authority to Scripture, but because of the illumination their work was capable of bringing to Scripture. However, the visible church in any age was recognised as liable to error and continually in need of being brought back to its gospel centre.

Canon Arthur Middleton shared the presentation of the 2012 Leaders Conference seminar on Anglican Ecclesiology with Dr Null and presents an Anglo-Catholic 'Ressourcement' ecclesiology which sees the process of Reformation as completed and corrected in the vision of the Caroline Divines of the seventeenth century, whose thinking later resurfaced with great vigour in the nineteenth century as the Oxford movement. Here, the Fathers of the first four centuries of the undivided church are seen as the authoritative interpreters of Scripture and herein lies the genesis of the idea of Anglicanism as a middle way, avoiding later mediaeval and Roman Catholic accretions on the one hand, but avoiding what they saw as the narrowness of the Elizabethan Divines' preoccupation with justification. The contrast with Reformed Anglicanism becomes clear when Arthur Middleton writes of this Anglican vision that it 'maintained the Catholic notion of a perfect union between Scripture and Tradition or the Church and Scripture in that the Church's authority is not distinct from that of Scripture, but rather they are one'.

To evaluate the differences between these two visions of our Anglican heritage is beyond the scope of this introduction, though the words by which the Jerusalem Statement defines our core identity as Anglicans seem to point in the direction of the Reformed Anglican vision of the sixteenth century by privileging the specifically Anglican formularies:

> The doctrine of the Church is grounded in the Holy Scriptures and in such teachings of the ancient Fathers and Councils of the Church as are agreeable to the said Scriptures. *In particular,* such doctrine is to be found in the Thirty-nine Articles of Religion, the Book of Common Prayer and the Ordinal [italics added].

Whatever vision of Anglican heritage we are working with, it is unlikely that there would be disagreement with Ashley Null's conclusion in his 'Anglican Ecclesiology: Summary of its History and Current Assessment' that Anglicanism cannot continue to rely, as often in its past, on promoting a generally shared morality as its mission. This allowed doctrinal differences to be sidestepped, but modern secular morality has infiltrated the Churches of the West so deeply that there is no common ground unless mission is now relegated to a kind of humanitarianism which is barely distinguishable from the work of secular agencies like the United Nations. Indeed, some Churches have taken the UN's 'Millennium Development Goals' as their statement of mission, and the Anglican Communion Office sponsored 'Anglican Alliance' relief organisation has chosen quite deliberately not to have a theological basis for its work. More than this the old structures of the Anglican Communion cannot cope with, and the rejection of the 1998 Lambeth Conference's moral teaching by the Anglican Churches of North America – and increasingly now by the Church of England too – means that 'the crisis over morality has destroyed the ability of any current instrument of unity to speak for all of Anglicanism'.

Morality and structures have failed and the only secure base to work from is therefore an ecclesiology which is built on our Anglican heritage. This requires a fellowship of national churches and a common statement of biblical faith, both of which we already have in the Global Fellowship of Confessing Anglicans and the Jerusalem Statement and Declaration. It also calls for 'a common structure of catholic order' and 'exercising between the national churches the ecclesiastical discipline implied in Article 19's phrase, 'the sacraments duly ministered'.' And all this is for the sake of mission. Let me quote the closing sentences of Ashley Null's article:

> In conclusion, "mission," I say, "mission." Mission in our hearts, in our heads, in our hands, in our hopes, in our failures, in our dreams, in all our lives and at our death, mission. For

mission has always been the essential DNA of authentic Anglicanism, since mission is the very nature of God's active presence in our midst as the church militant. Thanks be to God, our Lord will not rest until we and all that are his are revealed as the church triumphant for all eternity.

Professor Stephen Noll's essay 'Sea Change in the Anglican Communion' develops one of the implications of Ashley Null's assessment – that a mission shaped Communion does need some means by which the integrity of its fellowship of national churches can be maintained. Professor Noll outlines the way in which there has been a profound 'sea change' in the theology of the Anglican Communion over the past fifteen years and this has led to a 'sea change' in governance as well. Issues of governance cannot be bracketed off simply as church 'politics' which the spiritually minded should ignore, because governance has a powerful, if not always immediate, impact on our freedom to preach the biblical gospel. The breakdown of Communion discipline, especially since the ordination of Gene Robinson as bishop of New Hampshire in 2003 (a man who had left his wife and family for a homosexual relationship with a man), has been accompanied by the emergence of a Lambeth executive bureaucracy which marginalised the Primates and sought to supplant their decision making role.

The alternatives to executive bureaucracy are to opt for a loose association of purely autonomous Provinces or to be a conciliar communion of churches, the difference between the two being that 'conciliar governance involves common consent to an agreed upon deposit of faith and worship and mutual submission of elders in the Spirit'. Both the Primates Meeting and Lambeth Conference had in practice operated on something approximating to a conciliar model, but Stephen Noll describes how this came to an end in 2008 'The Lambeth bureaucracy proceeded to smother the Lambeth Conference – minus 280 bishops – with meaningless *indaba* interspersed by primatial addresses from Canterbury. The Archbishop made it clear that the Primates had overstepped their authority and would subsequently be confined to the plantation of friendly conversation.

There is however no need for orthodox Primates and provinces to be paralysed, faced with this situation. The Lambeth Conference of 1930 commended, but did not formally approve, a Report on the Anglican Communion which commended the conciliar model, and provides an alternative model which is biblically faithful from within Anglican thinking itself. From the outset, the GAFCON movement has been absolutely clear that it is not leaving the Anglican Communion to form a new communion. However, it is quite legitimate and indeed now necessary for orthodox Churches to clearly differentiate themselves from the old Lambeth 'Instruments of Unity' and reform Communion governance. As Professor Noll puts it, the movement should understand itself 'not as departing from the Anglican Communion but rather reconstituting Anglican polity on a theological, missional, and post-colonial basis'.

He then sets out what such a reconstituted polity might look like and over those specific proposals there would no doubt be lively debate. No doubt many in the GAFCON movement would agree on the negative, that the Lambeth based institutions are fatally flawed, but there might be less of a common mind on the shape of what model should be adopted for the future. A fruitful way of dealing with those differences would be to ask to what extent they go back to the differing visions of orthodox Anglicanism presented by Ashley Null on the one hand and Arthur Middleton on the other. The reconstitution of the Anglican Communion is an urgent task, but it is far from simply a matter of organisational redesign.

The seriousness with which Anglicans take history and culture, as seen in the Thirty-nine articles themselves, means that biblical work and reflection is never carried on merely in the abstract. It is significant that the second great gathering of the Global Fellowship of Confessing Anglicans is taking place in the context of East Africa, a region where church, culture and society have been powerfully shaped by the East African Revival. Colin Reed lived for many years in East Africa and offers an insightful account of the way this movement's characteristic emphases overlap significantly with those of the GAFCON movement, not least in its high view of biblical inspiration and the priority of gospel proclamation.

Archbishop Stanley Ntagali of Uganda has recently said that 'GAFCON is to the Anglican Communion as the East African Revival was to the church in Uganda. At first it was small revival fellowships meeting outside the church structures and church services. But, as the revival spread, it became main-stream in the Church.'[2] Colin Reed expresses a very similar understanding when he writes 'The leaders sought to transform the church from within, under the power of God.

---

[2] Press Statement 13th August 2013

So as we seek the renewal of our Communion we need to be utterly dependent on God, yet we value an organisation which enables us to act together, nationally and internationally.' The East African Revival is therefore a particular source of encouragement and inspiration for confessing Anglicans, a lived model in recent history which despite its imperfections was clearly a movement of the Spirit of God.

Archbishop Wabukala's address to the Fellowship of Confessing Anglicans UK & Ireland rounds off this collection. He spoke at a special meeting while in London for the 2012 FCA Leaders' Conference and it is a call to costly and courageous discipleship. In June the previous year he had ordained three young Englishmen in Kenya to serve as missionary clergy with the newly formed Anglican Mission in England in the face of fierce criticism, so his encouragement to costly faithfulness carried the weight of one who was prepared to lead by example. His words are a sober reminder of the reality of the spiritual battle and the false security of the middle ground, but also a wonderful reminder of the all sufficient grace of God out of which this movement was born and in which it must always live.

Revd Charles Raven, Archbishop's Officer for Anglican Communion Affairs (Kenya)

1. STATEMENT ON THE GLOBAL ANGLICAN FUTURE

Praise the LORD! It is good to sing praises to our God; for he is gracious, and a song of praise is fitting. The LORD builds up Jerusalem; he gathers the outcasts of Israel. (Psalm 147:1-2)

Brothers and Sisters in Christ: We, the participants in the Global Anglican Future Conference, send you greetings from Jerusalem!

1.1. *Introduction*

The Global Anglican Future Conference (GAFCON), which was held in Jerusalem from 22-29 June 2008, is a spiritual movement to preserve and promote the truth and power of the gospel of salvation in Jesus Christ as we Anglicans have received it. The movement is global: it has mobilised Anglicans from around the world. We are Anglican: 1148 lay and clergy participants, including 291 bishops representing millions of faithful Anglican Christians. We cherish our Anglican heritage and the Anglican Communion and have no intention of departing from it. And we believe that, in God's providence, Anglicanism has a bright future in obedience to our Lord's Great Commission to make disciples of all nations and to build up the church on the foundation of biblical truth (Matthew 28:18-20; Ephesians 2:20).

GAFCON is not just a moment in time, but a movement in the Spirit, and we hereby:

* launch the GAFCON movement as a fellowship of confessing Anglicans

* publish the Jerusalem Declaration as the basis of the fellowship

* encourage GAFCON Primates to form a Council.

1.2. *The Global Anglican Context*

The future of the Anglican Communion is but a piece of the wider scenario of opportunities and challenges for the gospel in 21st century global culture. We rejoice in the way God has opened doors for gospel mission among many peoples, but we grieve for the spiritual decline in the most economically developed nations, where the forces of militant secularism and pluralism are eating away the fabric of society and churches are compromised and enfeebled in their witness. The vacuum left by them is readily filled by other faiths and deceptive cults. To meet these challenges will require Christians to work together to understand and oppose these forces and to liberate those under their sway. It will entail the planting of new churches among unreached peoples and also committed action to restore authentic Christianity to compromised churches.

The Anglican Communion, present in six continents, is well positioned to address this challenge, but currently it is divided and distracted. The Global Anglican Future Conference emerged in response to a crisis within the Anglican Communion, a crisis involving three undeniable facts concerning world Anglicanism.

The first fact is the acceptance and promotion within the provinces of the Anglican Communion of a different 'gospel' (cf. Galatians 1:6-8) which is contrary to the apostolic gospel. This false gospel undermines the authority of God's Word written and the uniqueness of Jesus Christ as the author of salvation from sin, death and judgement. Many of its proponents claim that all religions offer equal access to God and that Jesus is only a way, not the way, the truth and the life. It promotes a variety of sexual preferences and immoral behaviour as a universal human right. It claims God's blessing for same-sex unions over against the biblical teaching on holy matrimony. In 2003 this false gospel led to the consecration of a bishop living in a homosexual relationship.

The second fact is the declaration by provincial bodies in the Global South that they are out of communion with bishops and churches that promote this false gospel. These declarations have resulted in a realignment whereby faithful Anglican Christians have left existing territorial parishes, dioceses and provinces in certain Western churches and become members of other dioceses and provinces, all within the Anglican Communion. These actions have also led to the appointment of new Anglican bishops set over geographic areas already occupied by other Anglican bishops. A major realignment has occurred and will continue to unfold.

The third fact is the manifest failure of the Communion Instruments to exercise discipline in the face of overt heterodoxy. The Episcopal Church USA and the Anglican Church of Canada, in proclaiming this false gospel, have consistently defied the 1998 Lambeth statement of biblical moral principle (Resolution 1.10). Despite numerous meetings and reports to and from the 'Instruments of Unity,' no effective action has been taken, and the bishops of these unrepentant churches are welcomed to Lambeth 2008. To make matters worse, there has been a failure to honour promises of discipline, the authority of the Primates' Meeting has been undermined and the Lambeth Conference has been structured so as to avoid any hard decisions. We can only come to the devastating conclusion that 'we are a global Communion with a colonial structure'.

Sadly, this crisis has torn the fabric of the Communion in such a way that it cannot simply be patched back together. At the same time, it has brought together many Anglicans across the globe into personal and pastoral relationships in a fellowship which is faithful to biblical teaching, more representative of the demographic distribution of global Anglicanism today and stronger as an instrument of effective mission, ministry and social involvement.

1.3. A Fellowship of Confessing Anglicans

We, the participants in the Global Anglican Future Conference, are a fellowship of confessing Anglicans for the benefit of the Church and the furtherance of its mission. We are a fellowship of people united in the communion (koinonia) of the one Spirit and committed to work and pray together in the common mission of Christ. It is a confessing fellowship in that its members confess the faith of Christ crucified, stand firm for the gospel in the global and Anglican context, and affirm a contemporary rule, the Jerusalem Declaration, to guide the movement for the future. We are a fellowship of Anglicans, including provinces, dioceses, churches, missionary jurisdictions, para-church organisations and individual Anglican Christians whose goal is to reform, heal and revitalise the Anglican Communion and expand its mission to the world.

Our fellowship is not breaking away from the Anglican Communion. We, together with many other faithful Anglicans throughout the world, believe the doctrinal foundation of Anglicanism, which defines our core identity as Anglicans, is expressed in these words: The doctrine of the Church is grounded in the Holy Scriptures and in such teachings of the ancient Fathers and Councils of the Church as are agreeable to the said Scriptures. In particular, such doctrine is to be found in the Thirty-nine Articles of Religion, the Book of Common Prayer and the Ordinal. We intend to remain faithful to this standard, and we call on others in the Communion to reaffirm and return to it. While acknowledging the nature of Canterbury as an historic see, we do not accept that Anglican identity is determined necessarily through recognition by the Archbishop of Canterbury. Building on the above doctrinal foundation of Anglican identity, we hereby publish the Jerusalem Declaration as the basis of our fellowship.

1.4. *The Jerusalem Declaration*

In the name of God the Father, God the Son and God the Holy Spirit:

We, the participants in the Global Anglican Future Conference, have met in the land of Jesus' birth. We express our loyalty as disciples to the King of kings, the Lord Jesus. We joyfully embrace his command to proclaim the reality of his kingdom which he first announced in this land. The gospel of the kingdom is the good news of salvation, liberation and transformation for all. In light of the above, we agree to chart a way forward together that promotes and protects the biblical gospel and mission to the world, solemnly declaring the following tenets of orthodoxy which underpin our Anglican identity.

1. We rejoice in the gospel of God through which we have been saved by grace through faith in Jesus Christ by the power of the Holy Spirit. Because God first loved us, we love him and as believers bring forth fruits of love, on-going repentance, lively hope and thanksgiving to God in all things.

2. We believe the Holy Scriptures of the Old and New Testaments to be the Word of God written and to contain all things necessary for salvation. The Bible is to be translated, read, preached, taught and obeyed in its plain and canonical sense, respectful of the church's historic and consensual reading.

3. We uphold the four Ecumenical Councils and the three historic Creeds as expressing the rule of faith of the one holy catholic and apostolic Church.

4. We uphold the Thirty-nine Articles as containing the true doctrine of the Church agreeing with God's Word and as authoritative for Anglicans today.

5. We gladly proclaim and submit to the unique and universal Lordship of Jesus Christ, the Son of God, humanity's only Saviour from sin, judgement and hell, who lived the life we

could not live and died the death that we deserve. By his atoning death and glorious resurrection, he secured the redemption of all who come to him in repentance and faith.

6. We rejoice in our Anglican sacramental and liturgical heritage as an expression of the gospel, and we uphold the 1662 Book of Common Prayer as a true and authoritative standard of worship and prayer, to be translated and locally adapted for each culture.

7. We recognise that God has called and gifted bishops, priests and deacons in historic succession to equip all the people of God for their ministry in the world. We uphold the classic Anglican Ordinal as an authoritative standard of clerical orders.

8. We acknowledge God's creation of humankind as male and female and the unchangeable standard of Christian marriage between one man and one woman as the proper place for sexual intimacy and the basis of the family. We repent of our failures to maintain this standard and call for a renewed commitment to lifelong fidelity in marriage and abstinence for those who are not married.

9. We gladly accept the Great Commission of the risen Lord to make disciples of all nations, to seek those who do not know Christ and to baptise, teach and bring new believers to maturity.

10. We are mindful of our responsibility to be good stewards of God's creation, to uphold and advocate justice in society, and to seek relief and empowerment of the poor and needy.

11. We are committed to the unity of all those who know and love Christ and to building authentic ecumenical relationships. We recognise the orders and jurisdiction of those Anglicans who uphold orthodox faith and practice, and we encourage them to join us in this declaration.

12. We celebrate the God-given diversity among us which enriches our global fellowship, and we acknowledge freedom in secondary matters. We pledge to work together to seek the mind of Christ on issues that divide us.

13. We reject the authority of those churches and leaders who have denied the orthodox faith in word or deed. We pray for them and call on them to repent and return to the Lord.

14. We rejoice at the prospect of Jesus' coming again in glory, and while we await this final event of history, we praise him for the way he builds up his church through his Spirit by miraculously changing lives.

1.5. *The Road Ahead*

We believe the Holy Spirit has led us during this week in Jerusalem to begin a new work. There are many important decisions for the development of this fellowship which will take more time, prayer and deliberation. Among other matters, we shall seek to expand participation in this fellowship beyond those who have come to Jerusalem, including cooperation with the Global South and the Council of Anglican Provinces in Africa. We can, however, discern certain milestones on the road ahead.

1.6. *Primates' Council*

We, the participants in the Global Anglican Future Conference, do hereby acknowledge the participating Primates of GAFCON who have called us together, and encourage them to form the initial Council of the GAFCON movement. We look forward to the enlargement of the Council and entreat the Primates to organise and expand the fellowship of confessing Anglicans.

We urge the Primates' Council to authenticate and recognise confessing Anglican jurisdictions, clergy and congregations and to encourage all Anglicans to promote the gospel and defend the faith.

We recognise the desirability of territorial jurisdiction for provinces and dioceses of the Anglican Communion, except in those areas where churches and leaders are denying the orthodox faith or are preventing its spread, and in a few areas for which overlapping jurisdictions are beneficial for historical or cultural reasons.

We thank God for the courageous actions of those Primates and provinces who have offered orthodox oversight to churches under false leadership, especially in North and South America. The actions of these Primates have been a positive response to pastoral necessities and mission opportunities. We believe that such actions will continue to be necessary and we support them in offering help around the world.

We believe this is a critical moment when the Primates' Council will need to put in place structures to lead and support the church. In particular, we believe the time is now ripe for the formation of a province in North America for the federation currently known as Common Cause Partnership to be recognised by the Primates' Council.

1.7. *Conclusion: Message from Jerusalem*

We, the participants in the Global Anglican Future Conference, were summoned by the Primates' leadership team to Jerusalem in June 2008 to deliberate on the crisis that has divided the Anglican Communion for the past decade and to seek direction for the future. We have visited holy sites, prayed together, listened to God's Word preached and expounded, learned from various speakers and teachers, and shared our thoughts and hopes with each other.

The meeting in Jerusalem this week was called in a sense of urgency that a false gospel has so paralysed the Anglican Communion that this crisis must be addressed. The chief threat of this dispute involves the compromising of the integrity of the church's worldwide mission. The primary reason we have come to Jerusalem and issued this declaration is to free our churches to give clear and certain witness to Jesus Christ.

It is our hope that this Statement on the Global Anglican Future will be received with comfort and joy by many Anglicans around the world who have been distressed about the direction of the Communion. We believe the Anglican Communion should and will be reformed around the biblical gospel and mandate to go into all the world and present Christ to the nations.

Jerusalem, Feast of St Peter and St Paul

29 June 2008

2. What is the Gospel

Seminar led by Dr Mrs Ngozi Okeke & Revd Dr Mark Thompson

The gospel is the life-transforming message of salvation from sin and all its consequences through the death and resurrection of the Lord Jesus Christ. It is both a declaration and a summons: announcing what has been done for us in Christ and calling us to repentance, faith and submission to his lordship. *'Christ died for our sins in accordance with the Scriptures, was buried and was raised on the third day in accordance with the Scriptures'.*[1]

Jesus himself proclaimed *'The time is fulfilled, and the kingdom of God is at hand; repent and believe the gospel'.*[2]

This gospel finds its ultimate ground in the character of the triune God, his perfect love and holiness. God will not ignore human sin. Sin leads to God's just and holy wrath and the awful reality of hell. The grave consequences of sin – guilt before God and the judgment to come, enslavement to sin and Satan, corruption and death – all must be dealt with. We cannot deal with those consequences ourselves, in part or in whole. In this light, God's determined love expressed itself most clearly when the Father sent his Son in the power of the Spirit to be the Saviour of the world.[3] *'For God so loved the world, that he gave his only Son, that whoever believes in him should not perish but have eternal life'.*[4] *'God shows his love for us in that while we were still sinners, Christ died for us'.*[5]

The gospel announces the work of the triune God. The Son came to do the Father's will in the power of the Spirit. By the Spirit he was incarnate in Mary's womb in fulfilment of the Old Testament Scriptures, becoming genuinely one of us while remaining truly God.[6] He was made like us in every way, sin excepted.[7] At the same time he is

---

[1]   1 Corinthians 15:3-4
[2]   Mark 1:14
[3]   1 John 4:14
[4]   John 3:16
[5]   Romans 5:8
[6]   Isaiah 7:14; Luke 1:35
[7]   Hebrews 4:15

the unique Son of God, the only saviour of the world. He lived the perfect life that none of us can live, always doing the will of the Father who sent him.[8] He died for our sins and was raised for our justification, always in perfect unity with the Father and the Spirit. *'For Christ also suffered once for sins, the righteous for the unrighteous, that he might bring us to God, being put to death in the flesh but made alive in the spirit ...'*[9]

The gospel, the proclamation of what God has done in Christ, is the powerful means by which God saves men and women today.[10] As the gospel is proclaimed, the Holy Spirit enables us to trust in God's promise of forgiveness and eternal life. Faith, genuine repentance and a transformed life are evidence that the gospel has been at work. Because Christ has died and been raised from the grave we cannot continue as before. In response to God's mercy in saving us, we are called to be obedient, to stand as Christ's faithful people in the world. We recognize that we now belong to the one who sanctified his people through his own blood.[11] Having died to sin in Christ we cannot continue to live in it.[12]

As those rescued by Christ, our thinking and our behaviour must be determined by his will expressed in his authoritative written word. Yet this new life of faith and obedience is never a human achievement. We are saved only through faith in Christ alone and even our faith is a gift of God.[13] We have been brought from death to life by Jesus and the life he gives us is life as it was meant to be, life to the full.[14] It is a life characterized by trust in God's goodness, love of God and of our neighbour, and hope in the midst of suffering, looking forward to that day when every knee will bow and every tongue confess that Jesus Christ is Lord to the glory of God the Father.[15] On that day, God's redeemed people will enjoy his presence in a new heavens and

---

[8]   John 6:38; 8:28-29
[9]   1 Peter 3:18; 2 Corinthians 5:21
[10] Romans 1:16-17
[11] Hebrews 13:12
[12] Romans 6:2
[13] Ephesians 2:8-9
[14] John 10:10
[15] Philippians 2:9-10

new earth in which righteousness dwells.[16] In the meantime, his service is perfect freedom.

The gospel announces God's great victory and the fulfilment of his ancient promises in Christ.[17] Sin and the powers that stand behind it are defeated.[18] Judgment is exhausted so that there is now no condemnation for those who are in Christ Jesus.[19] Death has been overturned by the one who is the resurrection and the life.[20] Exalted to the right hand of the Father, he pours out his Spirit on the church, equipping it powerfully to worship, to witness by word and deed to the gospel of God, which always remains the gospel concerning his Son.[21]

This same gospel, proclaimed by Jesus and his apostles, is our message in every age to a broken world of lost men and women who can be rescued only by Jesus, the crucified but risen Saviour and Lord of all. It is in the faithful proclamation of the gospel, and in the living of lives that have been transformed by it, that we give God the glory that is his due.

---

[16] 2 Peter 3:13
[17] Genesis 3:15; Isaiah 53:5-6
[18] Colossians 2:13-15
[19] Romans 8:1
[20] John 11:25
[21] Acts 2:33; Romans 1:1-3

3. A Global Communion for the twenty-first Century

The Most Revd Eliud Wabukala

Praise the Lord!

It is a great joy to greet all of you in my capacity as the Chairman of the Fellowship of Confessing Anglicans in the precious name of our Lord and Saviour Jesus Christ, through whom we are fellow citizens with the saints and members of the household of God. I believe that our time together here is a key moment in the unfolding purpose of God for our beloved Anglican Communion and it is a great encouragement to have leaders drawn from some thirty different nations as we gather here this evening. We are indeed a global communion for the twenty-first century. We have come together because of the Lord's leading as we follow His guidance towards overcoming challenges of our times and the continuing crisis which afflicts our Communion. I want to frame my address with some words of scripture in Micah which I believe are a particular word from the Lord for us right now.

Micah was a prophet during a particular time of crisis in the history of God's people, the latter half of the eighth century BC, during which the people of the northern kingdom of Israel lost their identity, and the people of the South, Judah, nearly suffered the same fate.

In Micah 6:8 we read:

He has showed you, O man, what is good.
And what does the LORD require of you?
To act justly and to love mercy
And to walk humbly with your God.

What does the Lord require of you?

This is the greatest question facing us this week. It demands that we have a clear headed understanding of the situation we face and are willing to let go of comfortable illusions. It also, and most crucially, calls us back to what God has said. Micah affirms that "he has showed you, O man, what is good". Discovering the will of God, what God requires, is not dependent upon our ingenuity or imagination. He does not play games with us. He speaks through the Scriptures. The question is whether or not we will allow the Holy Spirit to apply that word to our hearts and then obey it.

What does the Lord require? First we need to bring a biblical mind to the situation we face. None of us looked for this crisis and we may be tempted to think we can get back to a time when the life of our communion ran along more predictable and familiar lines. But that is an illusion. Faith is not escapism, but facing things as they are, in the confidence that God will act. The crisis we face is also an opportunity. Its origin can be traced back many years. The unprecedented challenges to Anglican identity forced upon us by the revisionist scriptural interpretation have, in the mercy of God, given us an historic opportunity to rediscover the distinctive reformed catholicity of our Communion as shaped so profoundly by the witness of the sixteenth century Anglican Reformers.

Trusting God's providence, we can be confident that in God's own time He is putting right what has been going wrong, but He takes us up into His purposes and if we are to understand the implications of this crisis for the recovery and renewal of Anglican identity, we must first be clear on what sort of crisis it is.

We cannot treat this as simply an institutional crisis. The breakdown of the existing governance structures of the Anglican Communion is a symptom of a deeper problem. It is now generally recognized that the instruments of Unity – e.g. The Primates Meeting, the Anglican Consultative Council, the Lambeth conference – no longer command general confidence.

Subsequently, when the Global South Movement Primates gathered in China last September they felt compelled to state in a communiqué that;

> 'the Anglican Communion's instruments of Unity have become dysfunctional and no longer have the ecclesial and moral authority to hold the communion together'.

If we were facing a merely institutional problem, then we would have expected that the heavy investment made in the Anglican Covenant would have brought a resolution. But now with the widespread rejection of the Covenant, even in the Church of England itself, it is obvious that institutional remedies for the crisis have failed and that the problems we face are far too deep seated to be dealt with by merely managerial and organizational strategies. As Primates of the Fellowship of Confessing Anglicans, we recognized in our communiqué of November

2010 that the Anglican Covenant was, I quote: '*Fatally flawed*". It had become clear that it was little more than a form of words to disguise conflict rather than resolve it. The heart of the crisis we face is not institutional, but spiritual.

Micah can ask, 'what does the Lord require?' in the confidence that what the Lord requires has already been revealed. But the Lambeth Conference of 1998 showed that a determined minority were willing to bend the word of God to fit the fashionable ideas of their cultural context and that they were not willing to stand in solidarity with the clear mind of the communion's bishops when opinion was tested.

The subsequent history of our communion unfolds from this point. Some sections of the Anglican Communion have been echoing the words of the serpent; '*has God really said...?*' (Genesis 3:1). And their strategy has been to continue this dialogue endlessly in order to wear down resistance while all the time pursuing their self-determined mandate of radical inclusion. In this they have been greatly helped by those Anglican theologians who claim that our identity is found in what they call 'the grammar of obedience.' They want us to step back from the plain sense of scripture and excavate 'deeper truths' of God's revelation concealed below the words themselves. It is little surprise then that we find scripture can be bent into all sorts of convenient shapes and that so called 'gospel' truths can contradict the plain meaning of scriptures.

While we should not shirk the hard work of biblical exposition, we can never disregard the plain teaching of the inspired text. It is that text that Archbishop Cranmer was so keen to have available in the English languages in every parish church, and translation of the scriptures into ethnic languages has been fundamental to the cultural transformation that the gospel brought in Africa and the rest of the world. The 'grammar of obedience' is a theological Trojan horse for profound disobedience. This accommodation to false teaching by Anglican Communion institutions has had a grievous effect.

Let me illustrate by contrasting our conference in Jerusalem in 2008 which launched the GAFCON movement and the Lambeth Conference which took place shortly afterwards.

In the space of a week we, though from many and varied cultural contexts, were able to agree and receive with great joy and celebration a clear statement of Anglican identity in the form of the Jerusalem Statement and Declaration. We rejoiced that through the

Holy Spirit the Lord had given us such unity in the truth and we knew that God was setting us free for a clear and confident witness to Jesus Christ in a way that was simply not imaginable through the traditional channels.

At the Lambeth Conference, which many felt unable in conscience to attend, it was a different story – much talking, but no shared mind and no attempt to resolve the substance of the fundamental doctrinal and ethical differences which have been so destructive to our unity. At Lambeth there was a loss of nerve and nothing more than conversation, but at Jerusalem we boldly reaffirmed our confidence in the faith we confess. There we recovered our genuinely Anglican identity and in the Jerusalem Statement and Declaration set out a coherent framework for global witness in the twenty-first century. The Jerusalem Statement, the preamble to the Declaration, clearly sets out Anglican identity. Let me remind you:

> We, together with many other faithful Anglicans throughout the world, believe the doctrinal foundation of Anglicanism, which defines our core identity as Anglicans, is expressed in these words: The doctrine of the Church is grounded in the Holy Scriptures and in such teachings of the ancient fathers and Councils of the church as are agreeable to the said scriptures. In particular, such doctrine is to be found in the Thirty-nine Articles of Religion, the Book of Common Prayer and the Ordinal. We intend to remain faithful to this standard and we call on others in the communion to reaffirm and return to it.

Our conference in Jerusalem was truly a mountain top experience, a rich time of fellowship in the Holy Spirit, of inspired teaching and prophetic insights. But we have to come down from the mountain top and not simply rest on the experience or think that by articulating a vision we have somehow done our work. What does the Lord require? He requires, says Micah, that we act, that we act justly and with mercy, not just write and think about things. We must act out of our God given identity, we must be true to ourselves as we are in Christ crucified, redeemed through the cross where God's justice and mercy meet. This is what it means to act with authenticity. It is not a matter of following our subjective dreams and feelings, but being true to the one who has risen from the dead, so that we might live not for ourselves, but for Him who died and rose again for us.

Living in this way is beyond our human capacities. In the words of the Collect for the Nineteenth Sunday of Trinity in the *Book of Common Prayer* we pray:

> " ... forasmuch as without thee, we are not able to please thee; mercifully grant that thy Holy Spirit may in all things direct and rule our hearts."

This for me is a personal truth. On being elected as Chairman of GAFCON/FCA's Primates' Council in April last year, I said this:

> 'I recognize that we have set ourselves a truly monumental task, but we serve God for whom nothing, not even overcoming death itself, is impossible.'

So we must act in obedience to what the Lord requires and, knowing our weakness, in continual dependence upon the power of the Holy Spirit. This is a truth which is particularly precious to those of us who have our roots in the East African Revival – a time when the Spirit of God renewed the church, bringing a humble walk with God: conviction of sins, a thirst for God's Word, a simple lifestyle and an unquenchable desire for evangelism. These are the qualities we need to animate our Global fellowship as we move forward together as a powerful movement of renewal and transformation, for that is what we are called to be.

Since 2008, we have acted, perhaps not always as quickly or as clearly as we should, but there has been action. In accordance with the Jerusalem Statement and Declaration, the GAFCON primates sponsored the Anglican Church in North America (ACNA) as a new province and ceased to be in communion with The Episcopal Church of the United States and the Anglican Church of Canada. It is a cause of great joy to see that despite aggressive use of the courts and the loss of property which previous generations intended for the work of the gospel, the ACNA is far from being just a place of shelter for the wounded. It is dynamic missionary body which is growing remarkably through visionary church planting.

Last year, it became clear that provision need to be made for England too. The Anglican Mission in England (AMiE) was formed last June after four years of discussion with senior Anglican leaders in England had failed to find a way in which those genuinely in need of effective orthodox oversight in the Church of England could receive it.

This week we will apply ourselves to discerning the next stage in what it is the Lord requires. I hope that our taking counsel together will lead to action that will shape the future of the Communion in profound ways. But as we pay attention to the great questions of theology and strategy, we need to be careful not to neglect the way we act towards each other, so that there is a consistency and integrity to the identity we claim.

To act justly and to love mercy includes behaving towards one another with honesty and fairness, as ends and not means, not being infected by cynicism and pragmatism that can creep in when issues of power and influence are at stake. It is true that the FCA is a prophetic movement and God has given us some stern things to say, but the sternness should be all the more striking because of the kindness and generosity for which we are known.

And all this we do with humility and prayer, not setting ourselves up above the word, but recognizing that it is the Word of God which judges and searches us. We shall also be alert to the fact that the word, which is God's truth for all cultures and all times, is not the privileged possession of any one culture – and a global gathering such as this has a potential to open new perspectives on the unsearchable riches of Christ.

To do what the Lord requires will also take courage. These are things we need to attend to if the Anglican Communion is to recover its biblical identity. The challenges are indeed monumental and I think they can be summarized as follows:

1. We must keep the glory of God and the fulfilment of the great commission at the heart of the movement. We defend the gospel because we want to promote the gospel. GAFCON was launched as a rescue mission for the Anglican Communion, but that is because the Communion itself should be a rescue mission. In particular we should be building global partnerships to encourage evangelism and church planting. We need each other, for instance the South can benefit from the experience of those in the North who have resisted and understand the dynamics of a western secularizing culture which is rapidly spreading around the globe. The North also can benefit from the missionary enthusiasm and vigour which is characterizing the growing Churches of the global South - we cannot be content for Anglicanism to be a kind of chaplaincy to dwindling enclaves of those who have been left behind by the receding tide of faith.

2. We should look to pioneer the new wineskin of the global governance structures which will help and not hinder the task of evangelism. Four years ago the Jerusalem Statement spoke of the 'manifest failure' of the instruments of Unity in the Anglican Communion, and since then it has become entirely clear that these instruments have failed us. Orthodox leaders must now do more than simply stay away. We have to go back to basic principles and develop new structures while remaining firmly within the Anglican Communion. We need to consider how we can build on the model of conciliar leadership initiated in Jerusalem in 2008 with the setting up of the GAFCON Primates' Council. Our Communion has come of age and it is now time that its leadership should be focused not on one person or one Church, however hallowed its history, but on the one historic faith we confess.

3. We must resist the temptation to be theologically lazy. Our aim of a renewed, reformed Anglican Communion will not be sustained if we are unwilling to support and encourage those who are gifted to do the training and the theological heavy lifting so essential to give depth and penetration to our vision. We need to recover the vision of the Anglican Reformers, of ordinary believers knowing scriptures and being nourished by biblical teaching. Equally we need leaders, lay and ordained, able to give a robust defence of apostolic faith in the global public square. If we do not, secular ideologies which have so powerfully shaped liberal and revisionist Christianity in the Communion will tighten their grip. The Lord our God calls us to move on.

So what does the Lord require? He has called us to a great prophetic purpose at this critical point in the life of our communion. After some 450 years it is becoming clear that what some have called the 'Anglican experiment' is not ending in failure, but is on the verge of a new and truly global future in which the original vision of the reformers can be realized as never before. We do not need to repudiate or belittle our history, but learn from it and set ourselves now to walk humbly with our God into the future and that hope that he has planned for us.

In the name of the Father, and of the Son and of the Holy Spirit, AMEN!

4. "Christ and His Body" Colossians 3:1-17.

The Revd Dr John W Yates, III

What a privilege to be with you this morning and to be given this great task of opening God's word with you. It is our sustenance and strength and so we turn together to Colossians 3.

Sometimes in Scripture it is the littlest words that make all the difference. In our passage from Colossians 3 it is the simple preposition '*with*' that plays this role. It establishes the radical theological claim that we as followers of Jesus Christ have been united with him in his resurrection and eternal reign.

Three times already in chapter two (vv.12, 13 and 20) Paul has described the Colossians as being *with* Christ, establishing the fact of their union. Now, three times again Paul returns to the phrase, unpacking its significance so as to lead this misled Church back to the power of the gospel.

Let me re-read verses 1-4:

If then you have been raised with Christ, seek the things that are above, where Christ is, seated at the right hand of God. Set your minds on things that are above, not on things that are on the earth. For you have died and your life is hidden with Christ in God. When Christ who is your life appears, then you also will appear with him in glory.

Strategic repetition of that little word *with* hammers home the astonishing reality that at the core of our Christian identity is freely received union with Christ. Out of this fact Paul makes four affirmations and issues two commands.

I want for us to consider these affirmations and then the commands, which will lead us into the balance of our passage with its specific ethical instructions. In verses 1-4 Paul affirms that in our union with Christ: We are risen. We have died. We are hidden. And we will be with Christ in glory.

Paul begins with the affirmation that we have been raised with Christ. That unsettling "if" found in some translations at the beginning of the sentence is a typical introduction to a conditional clause in which the truth of the statement is assumed.

We are *not* meant to wonder whether we have been raised or not. The paragraph begins with the assumption that this is indeed true.

For Paul to claim that we are somehow already risen is incredible. Anyone reading this letter will have no doubt as to their earthbound existence. And yet Paul still claims that we have been raised.

A brief look back at chapter 1 helps to unpack his meaning. In 1:13 Paul says that God the Father, "has delivered us from the domain of darkness and transferred us to the kingdom of his beloved Son."

To say that we are risen with Christ is to say that we have been transferred from the domain of darkness and death, and given new life under Christ's reign. This new life that we receive is *his* life – it shares his resurrection power and the intimacy of full communion with God the Father. As Paul says elsewhere, "the old has gone, the new has come."

To be risen with Christ implies that we have already died with him. This is Paul's second affirmation. The order is startling. Paul affirms that we have been raised and only secondly that we died with him. The affirmation has already been introduced in 2:20, "with Christ you died to the elemental spirits of the world." Our death with Christ is not physical, but spiritual. This is a theme known to us from his other letters. In Galatians 2 Paul says (vv.19-20), "through the law I died to the law, so that I might live to God. I have been crucified with Christ." In Romans 6 Paul says (vv.2, 11) that we died to the sin that enslaved us.

To have died with Christ means that we are dead to the spirits of this world, which no longer have power over us. We are dead to the law, which no longer can condemn us. We are dead to the sin that enslaved us but no longer can for its absolute power has been displaced by the Spirit of the one who died on our behalf. In our death with Christ we die to these things. To return to food laws and festivals, asceticism and the vanity of visions, is to attempt to inhabit a corpse. No wonder Paul speaks with such vehemence against such things. We are risen. We have died. Third: We are hidden with Christ in God.

It is the most unexpected of the affirmations in these verses and in some ways the most powerful. There are two senses in which we are hidden in Christ. The first is one of security and protection. The idea appears in the Psalms and elsewhere. Psalm 27:5 says, "he will hide me in his shelter in the day of trouble; he will conceal me under the cover of his tent." And Psalm 31:20, "In the cover of your presence you hide them from the plots of men; you store them in your shelter from the strife of tongues." When we are joined with Christ by faith he takes us to himself and hides us under the shadow of his wing. There no threat can find us, no danger can destroy us. We are secure and protected. This is our assurance as his people. And the power of this affirmation makes pathetic the false comfort offered by the heretics who count on visions, festivals and special diets for spiritual security.

The second sense in which we are hidden with Christ is this: we are hidden in the same way that a work of art stands veiled prior to the opening of an exhibition. The thought is reminiscent of Paul's profound reflection at the end of 2 Corinthians 4:

> Though our outer self is wasting away, our inner self is being renewed day by day. For this light momentary affliction is preparing for us an eternal weight of glory beyond all comparison, as we look to the things that are unseen. For the things that are unseen are eternal.

The metaphor is different but the meaning is similar. We are being prepared for a glory that outshines any we have ever seen. But it is presently unseen, hidden and in preparation.

To be hidden, then, is to be animated by a sense of anticipation accompanied by the absolute peace of Christ's protective care. What a remarkable combination.

Having emphasized the present reality of the eschatological age in the first two affirmations, Paul begins the subtle turn to an expectant future with our hiddenness. This leads to the fourth affirmation: We will be with him in glory. Scholars have long speculated that Paul did not write Colossians. Chief among the reasons is that the realized eschatology of this letter does not appear to fit with the anticipated eschatology of his other letters.

The argument might have some merit if in fact Paul's understanding of eschatological existence in this letter was thoroughly realized. But it is not. Here in this fourth affirmation that which he alludes to in the language of hiddenness is made clear.

Though we are risen and though we have died, we are not yet the glorious creatures we will one day be. The trials of this age will one day cede to the joy of bodily resurrection when we appear with Christ in the full glory of his new creation.

There is great comfort in this affirmation. Though the power of Christ inhabits us through the Spirit we are painfully aware of the limitations of this present life. Here we have the certain promise that one day we will be fully and finally transformed to reflect his eternal glory. We are risen. We have died. We are hidden. We will appear in glory. Four stunning affirmations accompanied by two commands. As always for Paul the indicative precedes the imperative. Who we are in Christ leads to how we ought to live.

The two commands are straightforward and well-known, and I want to look at them together: Seek and set your minds on the things that are above. These two commands have to do not with ambition but orientation. We do not seek to gain new status or possessions – they are ours already! What we seek is to conform ourselves to what has already been done and given – to live out this new reality with Christ. To seek is to long for, to gaze after, to search out. To set one's mind is to wrap it around the truth and then adapt to it. It involves conceiving, judging, submitting and creatively applying. Taken together these two commands refer to a fundamental reorientation of the will.

Paul contrasts the things that are above with the things of the earth. These are not so much spatial references as they are directional. They do not indicate that heaven is up and hell is down, but that the new life is lived when our new status guides us in a fresh direction.

Consider the contrast. The man who spends his life looking for coins on the ground grows old and stooped, curved in on himself and drawn down to the dust. Should he find unexpected riches he could not right himself to spend them. When we seek after earthly things we are quite literally living into the ground, seeking the dust of death and drawn slowly to destruction by the sheer force of gravity.

But when we seek after the things that are above we stand tall. We see above and beyond the horizon. We gain perspective. We live and walk toward future glory in the confidence of our hiddenness in Christ. During my first trip to the rural districts of East Africa I was amazed by the sight of women carrying water. I remember women of all ages balancing containers of water, some weighing up to 40 pounds, on their heads. What was most surprising to me was their posture. These women stood upright, they seemed to flow across the ground with a smooth and steady gait. They did not bend under the weight of their burdens, nor look to the ground beneath their feet. Instead their gaze was forward, their heads were high, their shoulders back.

We who have been given spiritual responsibility within Christ's Church carry heavy burdens. These are burdens that will crush us if our gaze is on earthly things. For a woman carrying 40 pounds atop her head the slightest bending of the neck means the total loss of her load. The same is true for us. The only way to carry our burdens is to stand tall, shoulders back and eyes ahead, gazing on the glory of Christ's reign at the right hand of God – drawing ever nearer, conforming ever more closely. He is our security and our hope.

The false teachers of Colossae had set their minds on the things of the earth. Through self-centred mystical experience, and senseless theological speculation, they sought to work their way to God. All the while they were missing the key truth that Paul is here affirming. We do not work our way to God, Christ takes us to him and there true life begins.

Paul begins with God, because we are present with Christ and under his reign. With eyes set on him and minds framed by his reign we turn to this present life and live. In these first four verses Paul affirms that: We are risen. We have died. We are hidden. And we will be with Christ in glory. These affirmations are accompanied by two commands: Seek and set your minds on the things that are above.

Having given these two commands Paul turns to address the rather more practical question: "How?" How does one do this and what does it look like? According to Paul it looks a lot like changing clothes. The rest of our passage can be divided into two. Verses 5-11 discuss a disrobing of the old self, and vv. 12-17 describe the donning of the new self.

Verse 5 begins with the wonderfully straightforward command, "put to death!" This command is followed by a list of 5 sinful practices that demand the wrath of God and must be destroyed: sexual immorality, impurity, passion, evil desire and covetousness.

Similarly, verse 8 begins with the command, "put away," and is followed by a second list of 5 sinful practices that are anathema to the one who has been raised with Christ. These are: anger, wrath, malice, slander and obscenity. Every one of these sins that Paul details are corporate sins – from sexual immorality to obscenity. One of the great lies of contemporary western culture is that what is done in private has no public consequence.

For a community that has been joined to Christ and is one in Christ there is no such thing as private sin. For sin not only harms the sinner, it taints the whole body as well. That Paul is primarily concerned with our common life becomes clear in vv.10-11. Here the evidence of our on-going renewal in Christ is the fact that in Christ there is neither Greek nor Jew, circumcised or uncircumcised, barbarian, Scythian or slave.

In Christ there are not merely new persons with new natures, there is a new humanity that is one with Christ. Unity is a fact of our existence in him, something we live out not something we create. Paul sums it up in v.11, "Christ is all, and in all."

He then shifts from the negative to the positive, from undressing to putting on fresh clothing. In v.12 he gives us 5 fresh articles of clothing, 5 virtues to replace the parallel sets of 5 vices in the preceding section. These are the virtues of shared life in Christ. Paul says, *"Put on then, as God's chosen ones, holy and beloved, compassionate hearts, kindness, humility, meekness and patience. "*

First, compassionate hearts. The Greek literally means "guts" or "bowels." It is a reference to the seat of our emotions. Although in western culture we now locate our emotions in the heart, the ancients were well-justified in locating them in our guts because that is where we feel it. To have compassion is to be so concerned with the well-being of another that you feel what they feel in your gut. If we are to live as Christ's united body this is the kind of concern we must have for one another.

Compassion is followed by kindness. Feeling must be followed by action – reaching out in response to what is going on. Those of you who are married know that over time it becomes rather easy to read your spouse. If you pay any attention to them at all you learn the little ways in which they communicate what they are thinking and feeling even when they're not speaking. This is a form of compassion resulting from intimacy.

If you are married you also know that compassion can be resisted! Inaction and laziness all too often follow recognition of the needs of another person. But the risen and ascended Christ expects us to act. Compassion leads to kindness, which is goodness directed toward another.

To take this kind of action on a regular basis requires humility, which is the third virtue. It is an essential article of godly clothing and yet so difficult to squeeze into! We clergy find this piece of our wardrobe especially uncomfortable, and so we try to custom-order a humility that restricts our egos only when absolutely necessary! How can one possibly learn to wear the humility of Christ? Dear John Stott had a ready answer that many of you have heard before, I am sure. When asked by admirers how he could be so humble Uncle John would reply, "Humility is just another word for honesty." And as they pondered the meaning of that statement he would add, "If you could look into my heart you would spit in my face."

Humility begins with naked honesty in the presence of our risen king. This humility begins to blossom in our relationships when we consider that the brothers and sisters with whom we relate are not merely siblings, but heavenly creatures whose future glory is so dazzling that they are now hidden with Christ as they await his return. The glory of Christ in the presence of a brother is a humbling thing indeed. Paul continues to dress us with meekness, or as other translations put it, gentleness. This virtue is closely related to humility, but the English word gentleness adds a helpful gloss. Pride can be violent – whether in deed or word, or the silent assault of a spiteful glance.

Family life in the body of Christ can be tempestuous and it is important to treat one another, even in the most volatile of times, with the utmost tenderness. That is gentleness.

And finally there is patience. It's the last thing Paul tells his friends to wear – and with good reason. Our unity is life-long. The road stretches out before us, and if we do not learn patience and practice patience the thread of these other virtues will unravel as we wear them. It is no wonder that in v.13, as Paul fleshes out the application of these 5 virtues, he instructs us to forgive one another as Christ forgave us. Patience comes to maturity in the virtue of repeated forgiveness. And on top of all these things we are to put on love, which binds them all together. When these virtues are present in the gathered people of God there is peace and unity of a kind only found through the work of the risen and ascended Christ.

Paul draws this section to a close by returning to the gospel:

Let the word of Christ dwell in you richly, teaching and admonishing one another in all wisdom, singing psalms and hymns and spiritual songs, with thankfulness in your hearts to God. And whatever you do, in word or deed, do everything in the name of the Lord Jesus, giving thanks to God the Father through him.

When Christ is proclaimed, teaching leads to singing, thanksgiving and praise. Worship and ethics go hand in hand because it is only as we grasp the gospel and are caught up in the glory of Christ that we will live with him, conformed to his life, which we share.

We need to conclude. When Paul wrote this letter the church in Colossae was in trouble. False teachers had infiltrated the people of God, leading them, as Paul so powerfully puts it in 2:17, to cast about in the shadows of religion while ignoring the substance of Christ. At the root of the trouble in Colossae was a sense of anxiety with the world and one's place in it. There was a hunger for spiritual security. The distractions and heresies promoted by the false teachers simply fed on those fears and insecurities, providing empty hope and cold comfort.

I do not know of any region in the world today that is free from anxiety. Whether one ministers in western Uganda or the west end of London, uncertainty abounds. There are thus few churches in the world free from the parasite of false teaching. As ministers of the gospel we must recognize this basic reality. And in the face of it, lead God's people out of the shadows of religion and into the substance of Christ himself *with* whom we are risen, *with* whom we have died, *with* whom we are hidden and *with* whom we will one day appear in all the glory of resurrected life. Amen.

5. Christ the Lord of His World

The Revd Dr Michael Ovey

The key note for what we are about to embark on really comes from Archbishop Eliud's talk last night, when he reminded us that the heart of our crisis is spiritual, not institutional. Please keep that in mind as we think about the uniqueness and sufficiency of the Lord Jesus Christ, particularly in the area of creation. With that, let's move on.

If you get a head injury in this country, or if there is some kind of neurological question about you, some kind of disease, there are all kinds of tests that get run in a hospital. Sometimes there are questions to see whether you're in touch with reality or not. Sometimes you can be asked which year it is. But another favourite in this country is, "Who is on the throne?" Now, if the answer is Edward VII or Queen Elizabeth I, rather than Queen Elizabeth II, then everyone knows that something is up. It's a very good way of knowing if someone in this country is living in the real world. Who is on the throne?

Now, let's put that question about who is on the throne in a still broader context. Who is on the throne not just in the United Kingdom or Rwanda or Kenya or the United States or Australia, and not just for today, but who was on the throne for humanity 1000 years ago. Who will be on the throne 10,000 years hence? And who is on the throne not just for humanity, but for the entire cosmos? On the throne over all people in all places for all time. That throne. Now, some will say that no one is on that throne, and I guess you could call them cosmic anarchists. Others will say that they, or their friends, or their pay masters are on the throne or at least have a turn on it or a bit of it. And you could call them cosmic pretenders. And what marks out true Christians and therefore true Anglicans is their answer to this question – Who is on the throne? Our answer is that Jesus Christ the eternal Son is on the throne. He is the cosmic Lord. He is unique. He is utterly central to the life of every man, woman and child, on the face of this planet now and in the years to come. And He is also sufficient. Please note that one of the ways we have developed this conference is not just to talk about the uniqueness of Christ, but also His sufficiency. And this is one of the themes we must draw out – not just unique, but sufficient too. And it is this question, the uniqueness and sufficiency of Jesus Christ as the one true cosmic Lord that I want us to explore now. And the passage that I want us to use in teasing this out comes from Hebrews 1:1-4; they are very familiar words, absolutely wonderful words:

> In the past God spoke to our ancestors through the prophets at many times and in various ways, but in these last days he has spoken to us by his Son, whom he appointed heir of all things, and through whom also he made the universe. The Son is the radiance of God's glory and the exact representation of his being, sustaining all things by his powerful word. After he had provided purification for sins, he sat down at the right hand of the Majesty in heaven. So he became as much superior to the angels as the name he has inherited is superior to theirs.

You'll notice that something that's flagged up for us there is the identity of Jesus as the Son, the eternal Son, the Son who – in the words of the Nicene Creed – is 'begotten not made', and the rest of Hebrews tell us about the uniqueness of this Son. He is a Son who reigns with his Father, in contrast to the angels who are created beings, chapter 1. He is the Son who is the overseer and prophet for God's household, in contrast to Moses the servant. He is the Son who is priest, in contrast to the priesthood of Aaron and his sons, Jesus is the unique Son. As unique Son, he is utterly central to us, and these verses tell us about the unique centrality in three areas: He is unique in revealing God, in His role in creation, and in redemption. That word 'sufficient' will come to bear on all three of those areas. In a moment we will work through those headings in a more detailed way, but before we do, let me make two comments.

First, stand back and think about Jesus who is unique in revelation, in creation, and in redemption. Does that not take your breath away! Do you not find your mind reeling at the sheer scale of what's described here, and do you not find your heart singing at the majesty and the grandeur and the splendour and the glory of this Jesus! What could be better than to know Him? What could be higher than to serve Him faithfully? My prayer is that each of us goes back to our homes and our ministries with a wider, deeper, broader, and higher glimpse of this unique and wonderful Jesus.

My second comment is this: If Jesus is this wonderful, this unique, this central, then think of the appalling emptiness of life without Him. Without this unique Jesus the Son, someone does not know God, does not know where he or she fits within creation, and does not know how to be saved. All the wealth and power this world affords will not compensate for such utter emptiness. And a Church and a

Communion which does not treat Jesus as utterly central is utterly empty too. It can have all the pomp, all the tradition, all the history. It may be able to trace its institutional lineage back to Archbishop Cranmer, back to Archbishop Anselm, back to Augustine of Canterbury and the apostle to the Gentiles, Paul himself. But it is this Jesus who will fill its life with meaning, purpose, and redemption.

5.1. Unique in Revealing God.

Of course it's one thing to say that Jesus is utterly unique; that's like being in favour of motherhood and apple pie. I guess even the revisionists would say that in some sense. We need to know in what ways Jesus is unique, and that's why we must look again at Hebrews 1:1-4 in more detail. The writer of Hebrews has put things very carefully. He tells us about the many and various ways God spoke of old to our fathers. The reference to our fathers is a reference to the ancestors of the people he's writing to, and the context is the Old Testament revelation. And it's clear that we are to receive those prophets as words from God. But the prophets of old are put in contrast with what has happened now, in these latter days. Then it was the prophets, now it's a Son. God has spoken through a Son. Then it was to our fathers, now it is to us. Jesus is the Son through whom God spoke. Of course this makes Jesus and the revelation of God utterly unique. To begin with, we have got to underline that God speaks through Jesus as a Son. That's what's being put forward to us in these verses. Sons share their father's natures, don't they? A human begets a human, not a rabbit or a toad, much as my middle son would love to have a toad for a sister. And Jesus is begotten, not made. He shares His Father's nature. That's brought out for us in verse 3 – He is the exact representation, He is the exact imprint (in Greek). Now this has got to set Him apart from the prophets who went before, prophets like Isaiah or Daniel. He's human of course, but He is God's eternal Son, begotten not made, who took human nature on Himself for our salvation. And, says Athanasius of Alexandra, for that reason only, He is that Son. Even an *indaba* group can't compete with that! Now, this is utterly wonderful, isn't it! How good is this? We have a Son, speaking to us. What better revelation could we possibly have? The One who knows the Father from eternity.

This means that Jesus' revelation is not just unique, but it is sufficient. We need know nothing more. It is final in that way. Now, let's work through what it means to say that God speaks through His Son Jesus. We Westerners are very inclined, very tempted to treat Jesus as a wise man, but only one wise man among many others. But that misses His uniqueness, doesn't it. He speaks as Son, and other wise men and women, whether you're thinking of Plato, Barack Obama or Oprah Winfrey, do not speak as Son. They speak quite a lot, but not as Son. Muslims have, they say, a prophet spoken to by angels. But that is way short of a Son who needs no angel to inform Him about God, but who knows His Father eternally. Nor is it like that sort of agnosticism that rightly emphasises how different God is from creation but wrongly concludes from that that we can therefore say nothing definite about Him. Because to our shame, we have had leaders in the Communion who do say something really rather like that: that we can say nothing very definite about God. But the Son knows His Father, and knows Him from before the foundation of the world. Jesus says no one knows the Father but he adds 'except the Son', and then, get this for comfort, 'those to whom the Son reveals Him.' Again, is that not marvellous! The Son reveals His Father. What is God like? Look at Jesus the Son, but, and this is crucial, only at Jesus. Because only Jesus is Son.

Now let's be very clear here: from time to time, we have heard people in the Communion talk about Scripture, tradition, and reason. Well of course it's right and godly to use our reason, and to listen to the tradition we receive from our elders who brought us to the Lord. Respect for our elders is an area where some of us Westerners have something to learn, or re-learn, and recover. But as we think about Jesus the Son, and the One through whom God uniquely speaks, we realise that there is a wrong way to use tradition, and a wrong way to use reason. Because I can use tradition as something up there, equal with the Scriptures which Jesus the Son has given and authenticated. In Jesus' day of course, the Pharisees took away from Scripture by elevating their tradition. In the Reformation, tradition was used against Scripture to argue that we contribute to our justification by works. Tradition properly sits under Scripture. It has to, because tradition outside the canonical Scriptures is not God speaking through the Son. The Anglican martyr Thomas Cranmer kept on reminding us of that in the 1540s and 1550s. It is, by the way, a pretty good litmus test of true Anglicanism that we agree with the martyr Thomas Cranmer on the supremacy of Scripture.

So let me ask you how you think about tradition. Particularly my African brothers and sisters, I have learned to admire so much about you during these GAFCON years. But are you faithful in not practicing homosexuality because of the revelation of God through the Son, or because of your father's traditions? It is important to have the truth, but it is important to hold the truth for the right reason, too, and the right reason is that God has spoken through his Son. Western brothers and sisters, I need to ask of you, or I should say of us, questions about reason. How often have we been happy enough with the revelation God has given us, provided we agree with it and it appeals to our reason. What I find about our Western culture is not so much to prefer tradition to revelation but to prefer our own individual experience, or the experience of the particular group or club we belong to. For us, all too often, we think it's vital that our experience and reason confirms Scripture. We are happy with what Scripture says on abortion or homosexuality because our independent reason confirms it. But that's not quite allowing the revelation of God through the Son to have its proper weight, is it. The great Lutheran theologian Martin Chemnitz from the second half of the 1500s puts it this way: Scripture confirms natural reason, not the other way around. Because it's Scripture that's supreme, because it revolves around God speaking through His Son, and that confirms or disproves what I think and what I feel, not the other way around. Again, it's a terrible thing to think the right thing for the wrong reason. I think all of us agree that the 1998 Lambeth Resolution 1.10 was a great thing. But what made it great was not that it was a victory for our tradition or our reason or our observation. The critical thing was its obedience to God's revelation.

Now my fear for us in GAFCON is not so much that at the moment we are in error over issues like practicing homosexuality, rather that we may have a curious kind of syncretism that is the blending of proper Christianity with something else. My fear is that we dilute God's speaking through His Son by putting something alongside that. Not denying it, but putting it alongside. Whether it's our personal reason, the tradition of our fathers and our elders, our personal experience, our theological sophistication, our culture's sophistication, consulting the dead, or the spirits. Sometimes that urge to a kind of syncretistic doctrine of revelation arises because we doubt that God's revelation through His Son is enough. In that sense we doubt the sufficiency of what God has given us here. But that would be madness, wouldn't it. It would be imagining that what the Son brings in revelation is somehow not enough. But who knows God the Father better than God the Son? No one. It's humbling to say that, but vital, isn't it. Brothers and sisters, we must be humbled before the revelation and the word of the Son, for He is eternal Son, and we aren't. We conform to His Word, not the other way around. Now that is authentic Christian faith, and it is authentic Anglicanism.

THE TRUTH SHALL SET YOU FREE

May I remind us of the opening words of the first Book of Homilies, and let's remember that when we committed ourselves to the Thirty-nine Articles, we were committing ourselves to the Book of Homilies too. *'Unto a Christian man'*, says the first homily, *'there can be nothing, nothing, either more necessary or profitable than the knowledge of Holy Scripture, for as much as in it is contained God's true word, setting forth His glory and also man's duty'.* One last thing on this: I'm a theological college principal, and we need to think what this means for the training of our ordinands. Do our curricula actually reflect the first Homily here? Do our colleges make our ordinands read the Bible cover to cover? Do we as teachers actually treat the Bible as this precious? Do we frame our courses on ethics and pastoral care on this basis? Do we frame our ordinands' understanding in terms of God speaking by His eternal Son? Do we recruit teachers who do not accept the supremacy of Scripture? Archbishop Eliud was rightly saying last night that he dreamt of a Communion where all people knew God's Word well. How will that happen without clergy who are steeped in it? Archbishop Peter reminded us that GAFCON is a global gospel movement. How can we be that if our clergy do not know what God has said of the gospel through His Son?

5.2. *Unique in His role in creation*

Now, one reason we need to stress that God speaks uniquely through His Son is that it gives some content to the next point that the writer of Hebrews makes. He takes us to the Son's role in creation. He is the one through whom all things are made and who sustains all things. You can sum it up by saying Jesus the eternal Son is Lord of Creation. But here's the thing: I think lots of people say this, but Lordship needs to have some content if it is it be true Lordship. A god who is deaf and dumb does not exactly have Lordship. What we have just been saying about revelation vitally informs and shapes what we need to know about Jesus' Lordship in Creation. And what a Lordship it is! Through whom is our cosmos made? Jesus the eternal Son. How does our cosmos keep going minute by minute? Who sustains you as you hear and me as I speak? Jesus the eternal Son. And to whom does this cosmos belong? Jesus the Heir. He is the one with the title deeds to all that is seen and unseen, because His Father has established Him as heir. Again, this is breath-taking, isn't it! Wherever you look in creation, Jesus matters. All comes to be through Him, all continues through Him, and all will be His, for He is the heir forever and ever, Amen.

Let's think that through. All that is comes to be through Him, so any account of our cosmos ultimately has to refer back to the eternal Son's original acts of creation and His continuing acts of sustaining. Going back to the Big Bang does not go far enough. Why is it that we can properly call our universe one thing? Why is it not just a jumble of different things with no relation to each other? Because it comes through the one Son. Why does it hold together? Because He holds it together. And marvellously, He does so even now, in a post-Genesis 3 world. We live in a fallen world, but it is not a world the eternal Son has deserted, because He continues to sustain it. One of the great things about us as a human race and the universe we live in is that we have the capacity to understand, and the universe is made to be understood. It is intelligible. Why is it that way? Because the Son created it that way, and keeps it that way even in its fallen state.

Now we rightly wonder what our race has discovered about this creation, this cosmos. Human knowledge is a great thing. It's not the supreme thing, but it's a great thing. And isn't this knowledge also a wonderful and striking instance of the Son's mercy? The eternal Son, in His charity and His mercy to us, not only made this universe to be known by us, He keeps it that way, even for those who despise Him. We rightly talk of God's common grace, God's kindness both to believer and unbeliever alike, but we can actually call this common mercy too. Not mercy in the sense that all are saved, please don't misunderstand me, but it is a mercy that the eternal Son sustains humanity so that we can know the universe, and sustains the universe that it can be known by us, rightly used by us, enjoyed by us. Is it not a striking mercy that a scientist who disbelieves may discover a drug that saves lives? Is it not a striking mercy of that eternal God that a poet who disbelieves can write something of exquisite beauty, and is kept in being while the pen goes across the page? Take the tube, go to the science museum, look at the wing that deals with computers. And you'll be amazed at human ingenuity and inventiveness. But we should be even more amazed at the eternal Son who graciously and mercifully makes that possible. And without Him, there is no knowledge, no beauty, no inventiveness. Our lack of gratitude across the world does not mean that a gift has not been made. But by the same token, human knowledge, art, invention, find their proper place in the universe of the eternal Son – their proper place, please note – as real goods, but goods to be seen in their rightful place. Again, just think of the breadth and the variety of things we have just described. This is grace and mercy and generosity from Jesus the eternal Son, on a staggering scale, continuing day after day, even to those who are blind to it.

Let's move on to the next line of what the writer of Hebrews has to say about Jesus' role in creation. Jesus is of course the eternal Son who is the heir of all things. At this point we are starting to move on to something much less comfortable. You see, an heir owns something. An heir is someone who comes into property, into possession, who has entitlement. And if Jesus is the heir of all things, this is a way of saying that the whole cosmos ultimately belongs to Him. That note of possession is there in creation itself – think of Psalm 24:1-2. *The earth is the Lord's and the fullness thereof.* Why? Verse 2 explains: *for He made it.* Now in all of that we realise that as we treat this physical world, we are treating something of which the Son will be the ultimate heir. And that should give us pause, not just in terms of how we treat the environment and how we love our neighbours, but in terms of how we respect the ownership of our Lord Jesus Christ. When we put the doctrine of creation this way, with Jesus as the King and Heir of all, especially in this modern world, this is going to cause outrage. If the eternal Son is the heir of all things then that will include you, me, and every other member of the human race. And it means we can't be the heir. And that strikes at our pride and self-aggrandisement in a number of ways. If Jesus is the heir of me, then I cannot act as if I own myself, I cannot simply say 'It is my body, I will do it with as I please.' I cannot say 'It is my life, I will live it as I please in terms of what I do for a living.' I cannot say 'I will fill my mind with the things that I please and the images that give me pleasure', because Jesus has every right to say I must fill my mind and my heart with His word, and not just because He owns me, but because He is heir of all things. And then the tricky one for Westerners, if Jesus is the heir of all things, then we are stewards of our wealth.

Just think what this means for Western individualism, with its idea of strong autonomy, that I belong to myself, that I have rights. Actually the stress ought to fall slightly differently in view of Jesus as the heir of all things. We rightly talk in terms of how appalling it is when atrocities are committed by dictators against citizens – human rights in that sense – but actually we must speak even more emphatically of human duty. Because if Jesus is the heir of all things, then it is His will and His call on me, the duties that He exacts, that actually will be the authentic mark of Christian politics. That's not a new thought of course. It's been put forward since the middle of the 19th century by the Italian thinker Mazzini: that if we are to think about what the law is, the law is to love my neighbour and to love my God. Those are duties, wonderful things, privileges, but they don't fall naturally into the language of 'rights'. Think then what 'Jesus the heir of all' means to our ideas of democracy and state. We live in times where people do think that a democratic state is the voice of God. That's the old Latin tag *'vox populi, vox dei'*; 'the voice of the people is the voice of God.' But Jesus as the heir of all things means that a democracy cannot behave as if it has absolute rights of ownership. It becomes a tyranny when it does so. It doesn't have absolute rights because it is not the heir of all. That necessarily puts limits on the laws even a democracy can pass or the claims that a democracy can make.

The democracy in the UK cannot rightly make laws allowing gay marriage. It can't, because that would be acting as though it were the heir of all things. I have much admiration for the Westminster model, but it's not Jesus Christ, although I think some people who live there are confused on just that point! And non-democratic states also make inflated claims. A state, whether democratic or not, can act as though its citizens and their wealth and children belong to it without qualification. It can act as if it's the true owner, but that cannot be right. Because while the state may have rights and responsibilities to its subjects (think of Romans 13), no state has absolute rights, because it, too, is owned by Jesus. He is the true heir. He is the true heir of the People's Republic of China, as He is the true heir of the United Kingdom and Northern Ireland, as He is the true heir of the republic of the United States of America. He is the true heir. And as I say that, does that not both warm you and actually relieve you? Think of the character of the eternal Son. Who would you rather have as the heir who owns you? A state, even a democratic one, or the eternal Son who humbled Himself and died for you? As these things go, my country is not a bad one to live in, but is it not marvellously better for me to be owned by Jesus the eternal Son, than the UK state? Yes it is. And so for you, too. It is beyond measure better for Jesus to be the heir of you. It is a privilege and it is a blessing to be owned by Him.

That said, Jesus the heir of all things can provoke a very different reaction as well. Think back to Mark 12 and the parable of the tenants in the vineyard. They see the son of the vineyard owner coming towards them and they kill him. Why? They are envious of the way he is heir, and they want to displace him so they kill him. Sometimes, and perhaps lurking behind all sin, we want to be the heir ourselves. Not necessarily of everything, but of something or someone. Not necessarily completely displacing Jesus or denying Him, but making ourselves independent co-heirs with Him. Writing ourselves into the title deeds, or there again making somebody else independent co-heir with Him. That's a kind of syncretism, adding in someone or something as a co-heir alongside Jesus, the One whom the Father has appointed to be heir of all things. It's not robbing Jesus of all His inheritance, just part of it. And I think you can see that with secularism too. Secularism has the idea that there is a zone of life where Jesus is not the heir but other groups are. My fear is that you can see it in churches and denominations too, where a human leader starts to look more and more as a second heir. And that makes us ask the question whether the Communion behaves as though Jesus is the heir of all things, or do you think that something else has sneaked up there with Him? Our history, maybe? And equally, there's a question we do well to ask ourselves. It can be so easy for our objectively truthful criticisms of, say, TEC actually to be motivated by envy at their success in displacing Jesus as heir. Do you wonder if we are above suspicion in this question of envying Jesus as the heir of all things? That takes us to our next heading, and the last way that we look at the uniqueness of Jesus.

5.3. Unique and Sufficient in Salvation

You and I do feel a temptation to want to be the heir in place of Jesus; that type of self-aggrandisement is indeed close to the heart of sin, just as the great Latin North African theologian Augustine of Hippo told us so many centuries ago, Who is the better heir? It has to be Jesus, doesn't it? Because He is the eternal Son who was so humble as to take flesh for us and achieve purification for sins. This is the last element of this dense passage of Hebrews 1:1-4. Jesus the eternal Son makes purification for sin. Obviously this leads us into the theme that Bishop Michael will explore tomorrow, because we are moving into the idea of Jesus the eternal Son as Lord of His church. And really, as we think about purification, all I can do is re-echo what he has already spoken this morning: It is Jesus who makes purification for sins. Nothing else works. Nothing else is needed. And that's been at the heart of authentic Anglican theology for centuries, hasn't it. This is the simple Anglicanism that is based on the cross and on the work that's done there. I quote again Archbishop Thomas Cranmer the great martyr, on the uniqueness and sufficiency of Jesus' work on the cross and in His life in justifying us. This is the third homily from the first Book of Homilies:

> Christ is now the righteousness of all them that truly do believe in
> Him. He for them paid their ransom by His death. He for them

fulfilled the law in His life. So that now in Him and by Him every true Christian man may be called the fulfiller of the law. For as much as that which their infirmity lacketh, Christ's justice has supplied.

So, in conclusion, let's go back to our original question. Who is on the throne? It is this Jesus, the eternal Son, and the world knows so little about Him. And our first aim as a GAFCON movement is that the world MUST hear of Him. The heart of our crisis is not institutional but spiritual. Why? Because we have not yet done this, and brought the word of Jesus the eternal Son to all nations as the Great Commission commands us. And what a word to bring! Jesus the eternal Son, unique in revelation, and He is sufficient because nothing can be added to His revelation. Jesus the eternal Son, unique in creation, because there is no other creator. He is sufficient in that way. When you've said that He's the heir of all, you've said everything that needs to be said. Jesus, unique in salvation, sufficient because nothing else is needed. And the tragedy of what Archbishop Eliud calls the 'revisionist agenda' actually is the undermining of uniqueness and sufficiency in these areas. And when you have taken away the uniqueness of Christ in these areas, what are you left with? A vacuum – and into that vacuum comes human pride and the elevation of human beings. We supply our own revelation, we pretend we are the heirs, and we say we have saved ourselves. Archbishop Eliud was asking us last night, What does God require of you (Micah 6:8)? And that verse replies, amongst other things, to walk humbly with your God, without pride but with confidence. Confidence not in ourselves but in our unique and sufficient Lord Jesus Christ. The trouble with pride is our gaze becomes fixed on ourselves and our own glory. We are curved in on ourselves, we are '*incurvatus in se*', self-incurved people. But without pride and with confidence in Christ, our gaze is fixed on Him, and His glory. Is he not worth looking at? Christ is Risen! Hallelujah!

6. Jesus, Lord of His Church and of the Church's Mission

The Right Revd Dr Michael Nazir-Ali

We have been so ably led on the Letter to the Colossians, but I want to put before you in what I have to say three very short passages from the Letter to the Ephesians, which is of course a companion letter to Colossians. There are many similarities in thought and in context and even in the people to whom these letters are addressed.

The first passage is from Ephesians 2:19-21, which speaks of the Church as 'the household of God, built upon the foundation of the apostles and prophets, Christ Jesus himself being the key cornerstone [or perhaps it could be capstone], in whom the full structure [perhaps it could be every building] is joined together and grows into a holy temple in the Lord'.

So the Church is built on the foundation, the apostolic testimony. You may think – some people may think – that this contradicts what the Apostle had said in 1 Corinthians 3:11, that it was Jesus Christ who is the foundation. But actually there is no contradiction because the apostolic testimony itself is about Jesus, the apostolic testimony by the work of the Spirit points always to Jesus, reminds the Church of Jesus, glorifies Jesus, brings to our mind all that Jesus has done and said and is. *The foundation of the apostles and prophets, Christ Jesus himself being the cornerstone...'* Now the cornerstone is what aligns the whole wall, as it were each brick to another. And there's a cornerstone, over there, which says "1873": that is one understanding of the word that is used here – a very rare word by the way – or it may be capstone, the capstone of the pillars, that's the other sense in which the Greek translator of the Old Testament, the Septuagint, uses the word, something that caps what has already been put together. So Jesus Christ, I think we can say fairly, is both foundation and capstone: the foundation of the apostles and prophets, Jesus Christ himself being the cornerstone of the Church.

The second passage that I had in mind is from Ephesians 1:23, if you would not mind going back to this. It is quite an amazing statement about the Church, and it says about Jesus that *'God has put all things under his feet and has made him the Head over all things for the Church, which is his Body, the fullness of him who fills all in all'*.

So Jesus Christ is the head of the church in all things, not just in spiritual matters, not just in matters of doctrine or worship, but in everything he is the Head of the Church. There is 'no vacancy', as Mike Ovey was saying, for such a Head: that position is always, eternally filled, because Jesus is the head of the church, and we cannot therefore look to human authority, to human rulers, as claiming any part of that Headship. I think it is very important for Anglicans at last to understand this, and important that I, as someone who has been a bishop in the Church of England, say it.

The third passage that I had in mind about the Church in this wonderful Letter is from Ephesians, chapter 3:11, where the Apostle says that it is *'through the Church that the manifold wisdom of God is made known to the principalities and the powers...'* Through the Church God's wisdom is made known to the 'principalities and powers', and what are they? They are the assumptions and the prejudices and the principles by which human institutions and indeed the supernatural world are ordered and governed, or perhaps we can say disordered as well. 'Through the Church God's wisdom is made known...' This is a statement, if you like in the highest sense, of the Church's mission: to make known God's message, to speak truth to power.

Now when we read these exalted statements about the Church, naturally we ask: to what or to whom does this apply? And there are several senses of 'the church', both in these letters and generally, I wish to draw to your attention. First of all is that 'church', elect in Jesus Christ, which has existed from all ages, God's people throughout the ages and throughout the world as a result of God's gracious purposes for his creation. St Paul calls this in the Letter to the Galatians 4:26 *"Jerusalem our mother which is above."* That is the Church that is meant, not simply a human institution, but of and from the divine plan. Certainly that Church is meant. But Paul is very capable of coming down to earth, so in the Letter to the Colossians certainly there is this sense of God's eternal purposes being worked out among his people, but there are also references to local churches. St Paul speaks of the church of God at Corinth or at Laodicea or Rome or Ephesus or whatever it may be. This is the church in a particular town or a particular city as it is gathered together by God's will and the work of the Spirit in the life of the believer. It is a very important manifestation of the Church. So much of what is said in the New Testament is addressed to churches such as these.

But there is, I think, another sense in which the word 'church' is used in the New Testament. In his letters to churches in various towns – Romans, for example or Colossians – Paul often remembers the church that is in people's homes [Romans 16:5; Colossians 4:15]. Now of course the early church did often meet anyway all together in someone's home, but I think this usage is different. This means a part of the church in Laodicea that is at Nympha's house or a part of the Church in Rome which is to be found in Prisca's and Aquila's home or a part of the church in the home of Lydia or Chloe (it is interesting to see how many women are mentioned in this context). Each of these is properly called God's church. The church in someone's home clearly shares a likeness – people are like one another, it is a family representation – and this also allows us to express church where people are like one another, in interest or profession or ethnicity perhaps or language. I used to be rather hostile to people speaking of the church in this way, where the church is characterized by homogeneity, but I now see, from a more careful reading of the New Testament, that there is a valid understanding of the church here that is possible – for example, a church like that of Fresh Expressions: so many of the Fresh Expressions in this country are characterized by homogeneity. That is fine, but a church like that is not enough. It has to be balanced by other things. One of them of course is the diversity of the church in the wider community. In the New Testament it is a town: Rome or Ephesus or Corinth or Laodicea, wherever it might be. I suppose our parishes are not unlike these town churches, parishes like this one – such churches are now characterized not by homogeneity but by diversity. It is here that we noted both in St Paul and in the Letter of James instruction given about poor and rich together for instance, people of different social status; many of these cities were cosmopolitan centres, and so people of different races and languages, Jews and Greeks and many different sorts of people. So when we speak of the church, we have to keep all of this in mind.

When can we say, in this situation or that, that the church of God, the church of Christ is present to a sufficient extent that the Lord is among his people? Article XIX, which is appropriately titled 'Of the Church', says that 'The church of Christ is a congregation of faithful men in which the pure Word of God is preached and the sacraments duly administered.' And I think each of those phrases is important. If congregations (Ashley [Null] was telling us in his seminar that 'congregation' is merely a translation of *ekklesia)* are congregations of faithful men, however that may be expressed – in a household or town-wide in a parish church – the faithfulness, faithful men, faithful people (that is important), are people who have come to know the Lord, people who are committed to the following of Jesus Christ, places in which the pure Word of God is preached. How often we are told here in the Church of England: 'Vicar, you are going to keep to seven minutes, aren't you?' I think it is possible to preach the pure Word of God in six or seven minutes, but it is not desirable. And so 'sermonettes lead to Christianettes', as is so often said. The whole counsel of God has to be brought out. 'The pure word is preached and the sacraments duly ministered, according to Christ's ordinance'. That is, brothers and sisters, what makes the church, not a sociological understanding of community – though that's useful to have – not an understanding that relies purely on venerable tradition and place (I'm not saying those are unimportant) – but faithful people, the preaching of the pure Word of God and the sacraments. Without these things there may be denominations, there may be ancient traditions and churches, but are they any more the church of Christ? Or has the glory departed?

I was once at a very grand assembly of a denomination in the West, let's put it like that. It was very grand, very awe-inspiring. But in the middle of it, I had this sense that they had the form of godliness but not the power. You know what I am talking about. What makes the church has to do with the Gospel, that is to say, everything that the Church needs in its ministry – its life together, its preaching, the celebration of the sacraments – comes about because of the nature of the Gospel itself. In other words, how we are 'church' is not different from what the Gospel is. The Gospel produces what is authentically church. This is a lesson we must learn again and again if the ecclesia is to be *semper reformanda*: again and again to check how we are church against the Gospel – and you'd be surprised at how much resistance there is to such an idea in some circles if you put it forward.

Of course God provides for every church in every place all that the church needs for its ministry and its mission. That's the miracle, isn't it, of the work of God's grace. But it is also true that no church can be fully and wholly the church of Christ in a particular place without being in fellowship with all the other churches of Christ in all the different places. Of course, Jerusalem which is our mother above is that transcendent reality of the Church in which by God's grace we all participate. Of course the local church gathered together in the presence of the Lord, these are primary realities of the church, but the relationship between churches – Judea and the Gentile churches, for instance, the churches of Macedonia, the churches of Asia – these are also mentioned as somehow participating in the reality of becoming God's people.

At the time of the Reformation, some traditions, rightly because of abuse, emphasized the absolute importance of the sacred deposit, the Word of God in Scripture; others with whom we also have to do emphasized the importance of the sacred ministry. I think that it was something of a miracle in the Anglican Reformation that we were able to keep both together – sacred deposit and sacred ministry – because the Church needs both. We need that deposit of the Word of God once for all given to the saints; but we need also, brothers and sisters, the authentic teachers called and commissioned and empowered by God, for bringing that Word alive to our people, to make sure the Word bears fruit in people's lives, to share that Word with the world. Of course the sacred ministry is not on the same level as the sacred deposit. That misunderstanding can be ruled out at once. As is said in the Articles [Article XX], the Church is the keeper of Holy Writ, a witness to it, a steward of it, but always the church and its ministers are servants of the Word and not its masters.

It is true that we have to bring the lordship of Christ and the sovereignty of his Word to bear on our mission in the world, and this means really taking account of the world and knowledge of the world (philosophy was mentioned this morning in the Letter to the Colossians, science if you like) and to make serious attempts at relating God's Word to what the world has known in the past or is coming to know now and what it may come to know in the future. Anglicans have been distinguished in trying to relate God's Word to new knowledge, and we must of course continue to do this. However, we do need to say that revelation is about confirming reason. The priority of revelation must be maintained particularly when it relates, for example, to purpose in our world, to the meaning of creation, to human destiny, to human freedom given by God and so gone wrong because of us.

Any interpretation of the world – of the origins of human life, of the coming of consciousness and self-consciousness – that does not take account of why the world has been made, what for, and what our destiny is, must be judged inadequate because it does not fit in with the revelation that God has given us about his purpose for us and our destiny therefore in him. Now if we are going to understand how the church is and how the church relates to the world around it, understood in these different ways which I have tried very briefly to explain, what should the church be doing, to be the church? There are certain things that are absolutely essential for the church, in every aspect of its manifestation, to be and to do.

First of all, it must be possible for God's people to gather. To be a lone Christian is a dead Christian. We must gather together, must we not, to hear God's Word, to celebrate the sacraments, to learn from one another, to pray for one another – the list is long. Any failure at any level for Christians to gather together around the Gospel is a serious failure and weakens the witness of the Body of Christ. Gathering is so important, but gathering of course must be, first of all, for the sake of praying. How encouraging it has been here for us to be here able to pray together, to celebrate the Supper of the Lord together. It shouldn't really be remarkable for Christians to celebrate the Lord's Supper together, but in our Communion in recent years it has become a problem. Gathering together, praying together, learning from God's Word and from one another together – together! – and the learning has to be not just from one another, not just an affair that has to do with us, however careful the listening and however exalting *indaba* might be (I've no personal experience of it) it has to be around God's Word! That is absolutely essential.

And then teaching together. The Church has to say from time to time something about how the world is, what issues are faced by a nation or a community or the world. From time to time, it has to declare what God's Word is saying in this situation or that. Now the Lambeth Conferences have never been perfect – I have been closely involved with some, and I would not pretend in any way that they have ever been perfect – but until the last one it was possible for Anglican bishops gathered together in solemn assembly to speak authoritatively – whether that was about our relations with other churches, what we thought of other faiths, whether that was about the need for Christian unity, our self-understanding as Anglicans at the 1930 Conference, the coming into being of the Church of South India in 1948, the family in 1958, and then of course in 1998 on human sexuality – the Lambeth Conferences were able to say with spiritual and moral authority, even if not legal, what the Church's faith was. But that has become impossible now. This is a serious injury to the Body, the inability to keep together and the keeping together of course comes about not only as result of consulting and learning together but of deciding together. In the 'Appeal to All Christian People' in 1920, the church decided together – the bishops together decided – on what terms Anglicans would be willing to talk about unity with other Christians, and that became useful not just for Anglicans but for all sorts of other Christians as well. In 1998 the bishops gathered together and by a huge majority, an overwhelming majority, decided together that they would teach in their own dioceses and provinces what they had discerned to be God's will in terms of human sexual behaviour, deciding how important that is for our life together.

But then of course there is the will to discipline, which arises out of the common decision-making and the common teaching that the church is able to declare in the world. There was a big debate at the time of the Reformation about what place discipline should have in the church, and the Reformers were rightly wary of the excessive discipline of the medieval church. But the Anglican Reformers, as is well set out in the Second Book of Homilies [Book 2, Homily 16 for Whitsunday], make it quite clear that the Anglican tradition is for effective discipline in the Church. It is not that the church cannot exist without discipline, but that the church's good, the church's spiritual good, comes about through effective discipline in the Body. This ought to be obvious: any institution, even human institutions, cannot function without discipline. How do we expect the church of God, so diverse, with people from so many different backgrounds and issues and gifts, to function without discipline?

Well, if that's the case, brothers and sisters, what could we be saying about our Anglican Communion today? It has been said already that the so-called Instruments of Communion that have developed over the last fifty years or so have all failed in one way or another. Even the Lambeth Conference that has existed for a much longer period than that, has been found not to be effective in setting forth the teaching of God's Word as we understand it in the situation that men and women face in their particular context. Now in this I don't think the Instruments can be given artificial respiration and somehow revived. It's been tried, and it may even be worth trying, but it hasn't worked. I am sad about that, but I think we do need to find new ways of association, of coming together, not just to be warm and well-filled, but to do the essential tasks.

It was successive Lambeth Conferences up to 2008, but excluding 2008, that said that the heads of the church, the Primates, have a particular role in maintaining the unity of the Church. Now both Lambeth 2008, the Anglican Consultative Council, and the progressive watering down of the Covenant have reduced, almost eliminated, the Primates from this particular role that other Lambeth Conferences were saying it was necessary for them to fulfil. I think that is a tragedy, because at one stroke it has made decision-making impossible. But I do feel that in addition to the Primates' meeting – in a way the Primates' meeting arises from what I am going to say next – I feel that what we need to be doing is to have a meeting of bishops, clergy and laypeople that comes together for consultation, for prayer, for identifying the issues and the opportunities that we have in our world, it comes together synodally – I'm not saying "synodically," – synodally, let's just say with the intention of walking together, walking in the way of the Lord. I hope that GAFCON 2 will be very much that, walking together in God's way for God's work according to God's Word.

But within such a synodal and missional gathering, there must be a gathering of those who have oversight. I'm purposely avoiding the word bishops here, because it would be easy for me to say such a gathering should be a gathering of bishops. Bishops should certainly be included, but I think we've got to move beyond that to a gathering of people beside the bishop, in addition to the bishops, who also exercise one kind of oversight or another. That may be in the formation of people for Christian ministry; it may be people who are rectors of churches that are crucial to the future of our Communion. (Rectors of churches like this one [St Mark's, Battersea Rise] exercise enormous oversight and have very large staff which can be quite well compared to what happens in a diocese. Why should they be excluded from such a gathering?). It may be leaders in church planting ministries. This will certainly need a reform of *episcope* in the Church, perhaps even of the episcopate.

Now I know what I am saying is radical, and there will be natural Anglican resistance to it, even in my own mind some resistance, but I think in all fairness I must say it. I believe that in associating in these ways will make us more attuned to what actually God is saying to the churches – the local churches, the clusters of churches, you can call them if you want – and how God wants to glorify his church, the church as she is in his eternal plan and eternal sovereignty.

How do we go about it? I think it is here that the Fellowship of Confessing Anglicans has a splendid opportunity to model this in our own life together as it emerges. That is to say, we do not to wait forever for non-existent Instruments of decision-making to make decisions that they will never make. You know, I'm tired of waiting. And you can't say I haven't had patience. But how long will this carry on? We have got to start doing this in our own life. So I'm hoping that the Fellowship of Confessing Anglicans will begin to show us how the Church is to gather, how to pray together, how to decide together, what to teach and also how we include people and also sometimes sadly have to exclude people, for the sake of discipline. Exclusion, by the way, is real in the New Testament but always for the sake of restoration, always for the sake of restoration.

Practically, I think what this will mean at our next meeting, God willing, when it takes place next year, is to have a mechanism that brings together people with oversight. I am quite willing to talk about how that may happen, how difficulties might be overcome, who would be included and who shouldn't, and all that can be talked about, but we shouldn't miss this opportunity because, in addition to the bishops, there are other people who can contribute to our gathering, praying, deciding and teaching, which is so important for us, and, what is more, when they go back to wherever they are exercising oversight they can make it real. We must make sure that this takes place in the wider context of the church gathered. I've always thought that Acts 15 is a very good example of how the church should gather. The whole church gathered, the apostles speak, the apostles and the elders set out what the decisions of the church are, and then the whole church sends out the message that it wants to send out to the world.

So for purposes that have to do with our next meeting, there must be a wide gathering of fellowship of listening to God's Word together, of praying together, consulting together, but in that context, those with oversight must have a special responsibility for setting out what we believe to be necessary for the future. And the Primates of course in their meeting will enable us to gather, to do these things and, later on of course, to implement what decisions have been made.

Now I am not saying that this should happen as a replacement for the Anglican Communion (God forbid!), but I am saying that this should be a model, a lesson that can be learnt by the wider church.

Finally, we must of course remain a dynamic movement, a movement that is committed to the Jerusalem Declaration. Some structures are necessary even for movements. Living beings move, and there are some very simple living beings that don't have very much of a structure, but a lively, developed and progressive movement needs some structure. I don't deny that; however, we must not forget that we are a movement in mission, and this may necessitate the inclusion of some people in our common life who do not belong to the structure, who are not people who are exercising oversight, who are not bishops or

Primates or rectors of churches, or principals of theological colleges, but who are leaders in mission.

In my time as a bishop both in Pakistan and as a bishop in England I have emphasized the voluntary principle in the life of the Church. Of course there are some things that the church must do officially, but the growing edge of the Church, the spread of the Gospel, the coming of people to faith, their growth and their nurture in the faith, often comes about from people who have been called to fulfil a particular vocation. Sometimes it means recognition and commissioning by the Church, but sometimes it just goes on, and we have to safeguard this voluntary principle. Paul Perkin was commenting at the beginning of this conference about the relationship of this church [St Mark's Battersea Rise] to CMS [the Church Missionary Society]. Well, CMS was a voluntary movement by people called by God to fulfil a certain vision, just as the Clapham sect generally and locally here was called to fulfil that mission. I often say that when CMS was formed, it wrote to the Archbishop of Canterbury, seeking his blessing, and it took two years for the Archbishop of Canterbury even to reply. But that did not stop it from doing what it had to do, and we must be praying that God will produce, as indeed he has, movements in our Anglican Communion, in our local churches, in our national churches, for bringing people to faith, for renewal in the life of the Church, for leadership in worship, and that we shouldn't be suspicious of these movements as if they were harmful for the institutions, but celebrate them as God's gift to us today. Effective leadership, effective *episcope* if you like, exercised now by Primates and bishops, but I think part of that for the future must be recognition of, and enabling of and empowering of, this voluntary principle, in that light once again we can learn from our past.

We can be confident of Christ's Lordship in a Church which is faithful to his Word and which seeks to bring this Word to bear on the needs, aspirations, fears and hopes of the world to which it has been sent as an ambassador. Let us humbly, but properly, recover our confidence in the transforming power of God's Word.

7. Sixteenth Century Anglican Ecclesiology

The Revd Dr Ashley Null

Based on the novel by Nicholas Sparks, *The Notebook* (2004) is a romantic film about a wonderfully obsessive love.[1] The plot starts off with an old man in a nursing home reading a story from an old battered notebook to an equally elderly woman each day. At first she is hesitant to be with this stranger, no matter how kind he is. However, as he begins to read through the story of young working-class Noah Calhoun and his doggedly enduring pursuit of the privileged but sweet Allie Nelson, she is initially intrigued, then enthralled. She always asks him to go on. The notebook's narrative charts the ups and downs of Allie and Noah's courtship—his initial daredevil stunt on a Ferris wheel to get her attention, their growing utter joy in being in each other's company, their incredibly painful estrangement because of parental shenanigans and the difficult obstacles that had to be overcome before their eventual reunion, leading finally to their marriage and wonderful life together. Gradually, as time goes on, it becomes increasingly clear that the notebook is the elderly woman's own story about their story, her life with the elderly man reading to her, a story she herself wrote down in that very notebook but cannot now remember because of her Alzheimer's. That is why the old man is reading it to her with such tender, doggedly enduring devotion and love. Eventually, the moment comes for which Noah has been waiting. Allie's eyes awaken, and she says, "How long do we have?" Noah replies, "We had five minutes last time." "I want to dance. Hold me close once again," Allie asks. Noah takes her in his arms, and they slowly dance—the very picture of recovery of self at last, of finally coming home again, of inner peace finally found, of a long journey finally completed. But after a few splendid minutes of mutual rapture, enjoying the utter joy of once again mutually knowing one another's company, Allie cries out, "Who is this stranger grabbing me?" Noah bites his finger in angst. Paradise regained only to be lost again.

What a wonderful allegory of the human condition in general. Deceived by the foggy lies of human nature's millennia-long struggle

---

[1]   Nicholas Sparks, *The Notebook* (New York: Warner Books, 1996)

with spiritual Alzheimer's, we find ourselves driven to push away from our Creator and his life-giving love, the One in whose arms alone we finally feel at home. Only the direct, on-going intervention of his heavenly wooing has the power periodically to break through our confused haze. By telling us once again the story of his dogged pursuit of a relationship with us, he calls forth from deep within us the recognition that his story is our story and so restores us to our true selves in his loving embrace. For the English Reformers, at the very heart of what it means to be church is being God's instrument through which he woos each generation in their own language in their own cultural context to love him and one another because of God's great, prior love for them.

7.1. *Part One: The Visible Church as Human Institution*

For Thomas Cranmer, this divine wooing took place in a church which was clearly "a creature," but the Gospel was the very "voice of God."[2] As Archbishop of Canterbury under Edward VI, Cranmer oversaw the writing of a new set of formularies for the Church of England which clearly enshrined this ecclesiology at the very heart of Anglicanism's self-understanding. The *Book of Homilies* (1547), the *Book of Common Prayer* and *Ordinal* (1549, 1550 and 1552) as well as the Forty-Two *Articles of Religion* (1553) all looked to the proclamation of Scripture as the church's chief mission, for its message was the only antidote for humanity's spiritual Alzheimer's. So to understand the beginnings of Anglican ecclesiology, we need to look at the sixteenth-century formularies to see how they describe being church. But, before we do, we need to understand a few fundamental assumptions of the English Reformers.

Firstly, who is catholic? The English Reformers did not see themselves as Protestants, i.e., as a second, different branch of Christianity. There was only one catholic and apostolic church. There could be none other. And they, the reformers of England, were amongst its true members, but the pope and his corrupt hierarchy weren't. The purpose of the Reformation was to restore the catholic apostolic character of the church, not to replace it with something new. For them the phrase "Reformed Catholic" was a tautology. Only by reforming the

---

[2] British Library Royal MS 7.B.XI, fol. 32v-33r.

church could it be Catholic. Those who did not reform the medieval church were simply not Catholic Christians in the eyes of the English Reformers.

Secondly, the visible versus the invisible church. Because the English Reformers saw themselves as true Catholics, they never questioned the post-Constantine assumption that "catholic" meant everybody in a Christian country would belong to the same church in that country, the one catholic church. Where they differed with Rome, however, is how they understand that one church. The Roman church identified the institutional church directly with God's beach head of the kingdom of God on earth. The Reformers, however, rejected that identification. Let's look at the Nicene Creed as found in the 1662 Prayer Book. Notice that the word "holy" is left out when describing the church. There were textual arguments, since disproven, which thought "holy" was a later insertion.[3] However, the rejection of the word "holy" fits well with the Reformers estimation of the institutional church as primarily a human institution, through which God worked, rather than a divine institution in which humans were specially anointed to work.

In their eyes, nothing proved the "humanness" of the institutional church as much as a simple trip to Renaissance Rome, where the pope was as much as a secular ruler of a petty Italian fiefdom as ruler of an international spiritual dominion. Alexander VI—the Borgia Pope, Julius II breaching the walls of a recalcitrant city in shining silver armour, the breath-taking beauty of St. Peter's new basilica paid for by selling an archbishopric and indulgences to boot. Sleaze in spiritual places is not new. Nor is sex scandals stemming from problems associated with forced celibacy for clergy and members of religious orders merely a twenty-first-century phenomenon.

Therefore, the English Reformers made an important distinction between the perfect, truly holy, mystical catholic church which would be revealed at the end of the age, and the human, earthly, institutional church through which God worked to call his mystical church into being. They referred to this distinction as the difference between the visible and invisible or mystical church. In short, they followed what Paul Tillich called the "Protestant Principle," the idea that there is a vast difference between God's perfection and human

---

[3] See John Dowden, *The Workmanship of the Prayer Book in its Literary and Liturgical Aspects* (London: Methuen, 1899), pp. 104-9.

endeavours. Consequently, the human institutions through which God works will always be subject to the idolatry of too closely identifying their efforts with his. According to the Protestant Principle, Christians must always be on the look-out to see if they are worshipping and serving their own agendas but in God's name. True to this principle, the English Reformers insisted on maintaining the distinction between the visible and invisible church. The former was a clearly human institution and the second the perfect community of which Christ was the head and only those chosen from eternity as his were members. Because no one knows who really belongs to God, the eternal church of Christ can only be invisible.

Thirdly, the visible catholic church rooted in human society. Because the church on Earth was primarily a human institution, rooted in human society, and because it was also catholic, i.e., incorporating everybody in that society, it was accountable to the divinely established authorities for regulating human society, like every other group in that society. This point is absolutely crucial for understanding the whole idea of royal supremacy. During the medieval period, when a person referred to the "Church", he did not mean every baptized Christian, he meant those who had taken special vows to join the "Church", i.e., clergy and members of religious orders. When a priest committed murder, he did not appear before the King's officials for trial. Citing the verse "touch not my anointed," clergy could only be tried for crimes in a church court accountable ultimately to the pope, not the king. One of the issues that got John Huss in trouble with the church authorities was his insistence that the "Church" included both laity and clergy. The reformers insisted on the priesthood of all believers, that baptism, not further, special vows, made a person a member of the "Church." To show that distinction, Tyndale translated *ekklesia* with a new English word, "congregation."[4] You will see that word used in the Articles. It does not refer to individual parish families but to the unity of lay, religious and ordained in one body as the church.

Fourthly, monarchs are divinely established to govern all human institutions in their society. Because the catholic church on earth was primarily a human institution incorporating everyone within the geographic area of Christendom, the Reformers believed it was to be

---

[4]   Henry Walter, ed., *An Answer to Sir Thomas More's Dialogue . . . by William Tyndale* (Cambridge: Parker Society, 1850), pp. 11-16. See also the entry "congregration" in the *Oxford English Dictionary*.

organized along the lines of the divinely established authority for the rule of human societies within that geographic area, namely, kingdoms under the realm of monarchs. Just like King David, European monarchs were to be responsible for promoting the spiritual as well as temporal wellness of their subjects. Henry VIII was always only the head of the institutional Church of England, just as he was the head of every other human institution in his kingdom. Christ was the only head of his mystical church which would be revealed at the end of the age.

Fifthly, the visible church, as a human institution, needs to be rooted in the particularities of each human society. Because the catholic church on Earth was to be organized along national lines, to be effective, it needed to reflect accurately the specific culture of that nation. And, of course, culturally sensitive began with using the language of the people.

Sixthly, so where is the Holy Spirit in this human institution? Obviously, all of this has its own logical consistency. There's just one problem, isn't there? What is that? If the church is primarily a human institution, where does the divine come in? For a church without the supernatural presence and power of God, whatever it is, even if it is catholic in its universal nature, it still is not apostolic. How did the reformers understand the apostolic nature of the visible, institutional church? What was the medieval answer? Apostolic succession—that bishops were especially anointed to be the font of the Holy Spirit for their generation. They were responsible for interpreting and communicating the teachings of the Church. They were responsible for ordaining clergy who were then through the administration of the sacraments able to convey the benefits of the Holy Spirit to the people. For Rome, apostolic succession meant that the Holy Spirit was present and active in the church. And if the Holy Spirit came through an unbroken line of specially anointed holy leaders, how could a layman, someone not even a member of "the Church" as normally understood, claim to be the head of the church on Earth?

Not surprisingly, the English Reformers rejected the Roman understanding of apostolicity. It seemed patently obvious to them that the failure of apostolic succession to ensure apostolic teaching, not to mention apostolic morality, meant that the whole concept was bankrupt. They refused to accept the idea that bishops were automatically either infallible guides to divine truth or the source by which the Holy Spirit was dispensed through the Sacraments. Whereas the medieval church looked to the Bishop for these two important functions, the Reformers looked to the Bible.

Seventhly, the role of Scripture in the church. According to Thomas Cranmer's "Homily on Salvation," the Almighty gave human beings the Bible as "a sure, a constant and a perpetuall instrument of salvacion." On the one hand, Scripture was God's chosen medium to tell human beings the truth about the world around them and the struggles within them: "In these bokes we may learne to know our selfes, how vile and miserable we be, and also to know God, how good he is of hymself and how he communicateth his goodnes unto us and to al creatures." On the other hand, the Bible was also the means through which God worked supernaturally to turn people's hearts to himself and the doing of his will: "[The words of Holy Scripture] have power to converte [our souls] through Gods promise, and thei be effectual through Gods assistence."[5]

Eighthly, the Reformers' understanding of church. Because the Holy Spirit worked through the proclamation of the Gospel to tell people the truth about salvation and then also turned their hearts to embrace it, the Reformers believed that the church was the fruit of the Gospel. First the Gospel, then the church. After all, Jesus proclaimed the Gospel, then came the disciples. The disciples proclaimed the Gospel, then came churches. Thus, for the Reformers, the only way to be church was to be committed to the mission of constantly proclaiming the Gospel. Everything else was secondary. Including an ancient tie to Rome and other countries where Rome ran their churches.

We need to pause here for a minute. Because we live in post-Enlightenment times, we tend to see Scripture only as a source of knowledge, not as a source of the Holy Spirit. We see it in rationalist terms, not in supernatural terms. If we do not understand this point, we can't understand the Reformers or our founding formularies. How can a king be the head of the visible church? By ordering the Bible be made available to his people. And, of course, that's just what Henry VIII did, and he had a great big picture of himself handing bibles to his bishops and members of government at the front of every one of those bibles to make clear how he thought royal supremacy worked. The Holy Spirit

---

[5] Ronald B. Bond, *Certain Sermons or Homilies (1547) and A Homily against Disobedience and Wilful Rebellion (1570): A Critical Edition* (Toronto: University of Toronto Press, 1987), pp. 61-2.

came to his people through the Bible, not through his own person. This is an unspeakably important point! Let's take a moment to listen to the "Homily on Scripture" talk about this turning side of the Bible:

> *The words of Holy Scripture be called words of everlasting life: for they be God's instrument, ordained for the same purpose. They have power to convert through God's promise, and they be effectual through God's assistance; and, being received in a faithful heart, they have ever a heavenly spiritual working in them.*[6]

For those who would "ruminate and, as it were, chew the cud" of Scripture, God worked through the regular repetition of biblical truths to engraft in them not only saving faith but also a steadfastness in the pursuit of personal holiness that would gradually transform their character to mirror what they were reading:

> *And there is nothing that so much establisheth our faith and trust in God, that so much conserveth innocency and pureness of the heart, and also of outward godly life and conversation, as continual reading and meditation of God's Word. For that thing which by perpetual use of reading of Holy Scripture and diligent searching of the same is deeply printed and engraven in the heart at length turneth almost into nature.*[7]

In short, the spiritual effect of God's supernatural agency through Scripture was the on-going reorientation of a believer's heart:

> *This Word whosoever is diligent to read and in his heart to print that he readeth, the great affection to the transitory things of this world shall be diminished in him, and the great desire of heavenly things that be therein promised of God shall increase in him.*

Hence, "the hearing and keeping of [Scripture] maketh us blessed, sanctifieth us and maketh us holy." Little wonder, then, the "Homily on Scripture" urged that "[t]hese books . . . ought to be much in our hands, in our eyes, in our ears, in our mouths, but most of all, in our hearts."[8]

With these things in mind, let's now take a brief look at the Articles.

---

[6] Ronald B. Bond, pp. 61-2.
[7] Ronald B. Bond, pp. 63,67.
[8] Ronald B. Bond, pp. 62,63

Article XIX Of the Church

The visible Church of Christ is a congregation of faithful men, in the which the pure word of God is preached and the sacraments be duly ministered according to Christ's ordinance in all those things that of necessity are requisite to the same. As the Church of Jerusalem, Alexandria, and Antioch have erred: so also the Church of Rome hath erred, not only in their living and manner of ceremonies, but also in matters of faith.

Not surprisingly, the proper proclamation of the Gospel through Word and Sacrament is basis for identifying a true catholic and apostolic church from one which is not. Because the visible church is fundamentally a human, rather than divine, institution, it can and has erred in its doctrinal decisions. Please note these two marks of the true church "Word and Sacraments." When Cranmer says "Word and Sacraments," for him they are two-sides of the same coin. On the one hand, the power of the Sacraments is made effective by the promise of the Word of God spoken during their administration. On the other, the promise of the Word of God is made visible by the powerful use of creaturely things.

Article XX Of the Authority of the Church

The Church hath power to decree rites or ceremonies and authority in controversies of faith; and yet it is not lawful for the Church to ordain anything contrary to God's word written, neither may it so expound one place of Scripture, that it be repugnant to another. Wherefore, although the Church be a witness and a keeper of Holy Writ: yet, as it ought not to decree anything against the same, so besides the same ought it not to enforce anything to be believed for necessity of salvation.

Since God has ordained Scripture to tell humanity his full saving truth and then worked through Scripture to turn humanity to saving faithfulness, church's chief responsibility as promoting Scripture's message and protecting its authority for salvation. Article 20 states that "the Church be a witness and keeper of Holy Writ."

As a witness to Scripture, the church had to make the Bible available to its people. It also had the responsibility of providing clergy trained to help people understand its message. Hence, the Litany includes the petition that

"it may please thee to illuminate all Bishops, Pastors, and

ministers of the Church, with true knowledge and understanding of thy word: and that both by their preaching and living they may set it forth and show it accordingly."

The Prayer for the Church during Holy Communion makes a similar request:

"Give grace (O heavenly Father) to all Bishops, Pastors and Curates, that they may both by their life and doctrine set forth thy true and lively word, and rightly and duly administer thy holy Sacraments."

The ordination service to the priesthood lists the first duty of a minister as being a messenger who teaches:

"And now we exhort you, in the name of our Lord Jesus Christ . . . to be the messengers, the watchmen, the Pastors, and the stewards of the LORD: to teach, to premonish, to feed, and provide for the LORD's family."

Those about to be ordained are encouraged to equip themselves for this task by devoting themselves wholeheartedly to the Scriptures:

And seeing that you cannot by any other means compass the doing of so weighty a work pertaining to the salvation of man, but with doctrine and exhortation, taken out of holy scripture, and with a life agreeable unto the same; ye perceive how studious ye ought to be in reading and in learning the holy scriptures, and in framing the manners, both of yourselves, and of them that specially pertain unto you, according to the rule of the same scriptures. And for this selfsame cause, ye see how you ought to forsake and set aside (as much as you may) all worldly cares and studies.

During the laying on of hands, the Bishop prays that the new priest would be *"a faithful dispenser of the word of God, and of his holy Sacraments."* Afterwards, the Bishop gives him a Bible, saying, *"Take thou authority to preach the word of God, and to minister the holy Sacraments."* Bishops are encouraged to be no less devoted to their role as teaching messengers of the Word. At their consecration, they are asked, *"Will you then faithfully exercise yourself in the said holy scriptures, and call upon God by prayer for the true understanding of the same, so as ye may be able by them to teach and exhort with wholesome doctrine, and to withstand and convince the gainsayers?"* After the laying on of hands, they, too, are given a Bible and told: *"Think upon these things contained in this book, be diligent in them. Take heed unto thyself, and unto teaching, and be diligent in doing them."* Clearly, the *Ordinal* envisions a biblically literate clergy.

Since the essential task of the church is to proclaim the Gospel through Word and Sacrament, in times of religious controversy like the Reformation, being a faithful messenger obviously also includes being a reliable determiner of what that Gospel message actually is. Consequently, Article 20 clearly states that the "Church hath . . . authority in controversies of faith." Yet, this authority is only as a "keeper of Holy Writ." In his private papers, Cranmer compared this responsibility to the executor of an estate who made his judgments based on careful study of the will's written instructions. Hence, the article declares that "it is not lawful for the Church to ordain anything that is contrary to God's word written, neither may it so expound one place of scripture, that it be repugnant to another." In other words, the church was called not only to promote Scripture and its message but also to protect the Bible's authority to determine its own message.

The church's leadership, like everyone else, must seek the meaning of the Scriptures through diligent analysis and collation of the biblical canon. Their task was to discern how individual components of the biblical witness complimented each other and fit into the divinely designed overarching gospel unity. No interpretation of an individual passage could contradict the Bible's inner coherence of free salvation through faith in Christ (Articles 6 and 11) and its fruit of a holy life as defined by biblical morality (Articles 7 and 12) and made possible only by the grace of the Holy Spirit (Articles 9 and 10).

Article XXXIV Of the Traditions of the Church

> *It is not necessary that traditions and ceremonies be in all places one or utterly alike; for at all times they have been diverse, and may be changed according to the diversity of countries, times, and men's manners, so that nothing be ordained against God's word. Whosoever through his private judgment willingly and purposely doth openly break the traditions and ceremonies of the Church which be not repugnant to the word of God, and be ordained and approved by common authority, ought to be rebuked openly that other may fear to do the like, as he that offendeth against common order of the Church, and hurteth the authority of the magistrate, and woundeth the conscience of the weak brethren. Every particular or national Church hath authority to ordain, change, and abolish ceremonies or rites of the Church ordained only by man's authority, so that all things be done to edifying.*

However, the church's role as protector of the Bible's authority to interpret itself did not mean that all practices within its common life had to be clearly based on scriptural precedent. We will talk more about that later. For now, it's just important to know that Cranmer made a decisive distinction between unalterable saving truth, divinely revealed in Jesus Christ and faithfully recorded in Scripture alone, and changing human traditions of the church by which the divinely established gospel message was expressed and conveyed to successive generations of Christians.

Therefore, Article 34 states that every national church had the right to "ordain, change, and abolish" ecclesiastical ceremonies, since such rites are not divinely instituted, but are "ordained only by man's authority." Consequently, patterns of worship should reflect "the diversity of countries, times, and men's manners" of the human societies in which churches find themselves. "It is not necessary that traditions and ceremonies be in all places one, or utterly alike." The only caveat to a national church's power in the area of liturgy was "so that nothing be ordained against God's Word." Churches could not shape their liturgies so as to obscure the message of the Gospel they should be proclaiming. Here is the title deed for an Anglican Communion catholic in its global scope, apostolic in being united by a common Gospel, and culturally relevant by being committed to constantly rethinking how to faithfully proclaim that Gospel to the ever-changing varieties of human culture.

Article XXXVII Of the Civil Magistrates

The Queen's Majesty hath the chief power in this realm of England and other her dominions, unto whom the chief government of all estates of this realm, whether they be ecclesiastical or civil, in all causes doth appertain, and is not nor ought to be subject to any foreign jurisdiction. Where we attribute to the Queen's Majesty the chief government, by which titles we understand the minds of some slanderous folks to be offended, we give not to our princes the ministering either of God's word or of sacraments, the which thing the Injunctions also lately set forth by Elizabeth our Queen doth most plainly testify: but only that prerogative which we see to have been given always to all godly princes in Holy Scriptures by God himself, that is, that they should rule all estates and degrees committed to their charge by God, whether they be ecclesiastical or temporal, and restrain with the civil sword the stubborn and evil-doers. The Bishop of Rome hath no jurisdiction in this realm of England.

We now end where we began our conversation this morning. As head of the visible church, the English monarch does not claim personal sacerdotal power nor to be a font of such empowerment for the clergy of the Church of England. Rather, royal supremacy means that the sovereign has the God-given responsibility to govern the institutional church, just like every other societal association in the monarch's realm, including the right to bring its clergy before civil courts for the execution of justice in cases of any criminal activity. Since God has entrusted the right administration of national churches to the divinely-appointed monarchs of each of those countries, the Bishop of Rome, the duly appointed sovereign leader of both civil and temporal affairs of a small Italian state, has no jurisdiction in spiritual matters beyond that state, just as in civil matters. Therefore, he certainly has no authority of any kind in England.

7.2. Part Two: The Role of Scripture and the Fathers

It is so difficult for us in the Twenty-First Century to get behind centuries of the Catholic-Protestant split and enter the mental world of the English Reformers. Two questions yesterday after my talk crystallized the problem. On the one hand, one person expressed concern that by insisting that the English Reformers considered themselves Catholic, I was suggesting that they had a different mentality from the Protestants on the Continent. Now it is true, that some Anglican historians have tried to argue that the English Reformation happened in splendid isolation from the Continent, untainted by thought of such figures as Luther and Calvin. By no means am I suggesting that. My whole work is to show such notions are completely untenable. Rather, I am simply making the point that was brought home to me in Germany. In Germany I am not permitted to contrast Protestant and Catholic. I must always say Protestant versus Roman Catholic, for I am constantly reminded that Luther always saw himself as the true Catholic, not Leo X. To say that the English Reformers considered themselves catholic is just to state the standard mentality of all the Protestant Reformers.

On the other hand, another person was concerned that I began my lecture with the Sixteenth Century. Did I mean to imply that the Reformers saw themselves as starting the Anglican Church, i.e., that they saw themselves as making a clean break with all that had gone before and starting afresh from scratch. No, how could they, if they saw themselves as the true Catholics? They were seeking to reform a church that had left its true foundations by simply returning to those foundations. They were not seeking to lay a new foundation!

Let's think about this. Who and what is a true "Anglican" is much disputed today. To say that FCA represents true Anglicanism is not an attempt to break with the past, but rather to reconnect with the past. Indeed, the Jerusalem Declaration seeks to reconnect with specific elements of the past – the formularies of classic Anglicanism – which others feel have been rightly superseded by different, later events in the past like the Enlightenment. In short, our contemporary debates are just like those of the Sixteenth Century.

Where could the reformers turn to buttress their biblical arguments? Was there a large and long venerated corpus of Protestant writings which they could cite in support? No, for Cranmer and his fellow Edwardians, there was no Protestant culture to form them. Let's think about it. When did Cranmer die? 1556. What is the single most important book for shaping the culture of Reformed Protestantism, i.e., what is commonly called Calvinism? Calvin's *Institutes*. When was the final edition? 1559. What is the single most important book for Lutheranism? The *Book of Concord*. When was it written? 1580. For the first generation of English Reformers, as for their Continental colleagues, the tools they had at hand by which to define their Catholicism was only Scripture and the Fathers.

I want to spend a few minutes trying to help us to re-enter the mentality of those who wrote and first defended our founding formularies. I think a convenient way to do that is by taking the catch-words of the Reformation, *sola Scriptura, sola gratia, sola fide* – a description applied to them by those who came after, not by the Reformers themselves – and then putting them in proper context.

Sola Scriptura.

Without a doubt, the English Reformers were gospellers, people dedicated to and defined by their adherence to the power and pre-eminence of Scripture with its message of the good news of salvation. They took seriously the claim of Erasmus that Jesus spiritually indwelt its message:

> Christ's images made in wood, stone, or metal, some men for the love they bear to Christ, do garnish and beautify the same with pearl, gold, and precious stone: And should we not much rather embrace and reverence the sacred Bible, which does represent Christ unto us, more truly then can any image. The

image can but express the form or shape of his body, if it can doe so much: But the Gospel doth represent and express the quick and living image of his most holy mind, yea, and Christ himself speaking, healing, dying, raising again and, to conclude, all parts of him'.[9]

They even quoted this passage in the Second Book of Homilies[10].

Because God indwelt his Word and worked through it to send forth his Holy Spirit, there was a vast gulf in the eyes of the Reformers between the apostolic writings of Scripture and the Fathers witness to and interpretation of those writings. Again, if you do not understand the turning side of Scripture, you cannot understand the English Reformers.

Yet, we said earlier that the Bible also had a telling side, and it is that function I want us to concentrate on now. For although *sola Scriptura* is certainly an accurate description of where the English Reformers looked for their understanding of saving truth, it is not an accurate description of how they looked. For the English Reformers looked to the Fathers to learn how to read those Scriptures to ascertain those truths.

Let's take a look at Thomas Cranmer.

The Anglican triad of Scripture, tradition and reason did not originate with Hooker. Why should it have? Hooker did not claim to be presenting an original construal of theology. He claimed to be defending the accepted principles of the Protestant religion as established in England. The first recorded reference that I can find to this fundamental tenet of Anglican hermeneutics is July 1539.

[T]he Archbishop collecting both his arguments, authorities of Scriptures, and Doctors together, caused his Secretary to write a fair book thereof for the king, after this order. First the Scriptures were alleged, then the Doctors, thirdly followed the arguments deducted from those authorities.[11]

---

[9]   Erasmus, *An exhortation to the diligent studye of scripture* (Antwerp: J. Hoochstraten, 1529), sig. A6r.
[10] See "An Information for them which take offence at certain places of the Holy Scripture."
[11] John Foxe, *Actes and Monuments* (London: John Day, 1570), p. 1355.

From the Fathers, Cranmer learned the regulative principle in matters of salvation. In his 1532 edition of Basil writings in Greek, Cranmer made a marginal comment: "Holy Scripture contains all things necessary for salvation."[12] He quotes Chrysostom to the same effect in his 1547 "Homily on Salvation" and, of course, the statement made its way into the Articles of Religion, the confession of faith that was meant to supplement the ancient creeds in giving instruction to Anglicans in how to read their bibles. Now what is the regulative principle? A key concept for understanding the role of Scripture in the English Reformation.

Regulative versus Normative.

Regulative means you have to have a clear Scriptural injunction– a rule, a reference – on which something is based. Normative means that it is a standard which cannot be contradicted. So for the Roman Catholic Church in matters of salvation, is the Bible normative or regulative? It is normative. Nothing in the Bible says Mary was not bodily assumed into Heaven so that church tradition's insistence on this point can be held by the Roman pope to be necessary for salvation. For the Fathers, Cranmer, and all the Protestant Reformers, the Bible is regulative in matters of salvation, i.e., *sola Scriptura*. But what about the changing human traditions of the church by which the divinely established gospel message is expressed and conveyed to successive generations of Christians. Is the Bible normative or regulative here? This question was the heart of the matter in Cranmer's famous disputes with the more progressive reformers John Hooper and John Knox.

In 1550 Hooper had refused to be consecrated as Bishop of Gloucester, since he would have to wear a surplice and cope, something he considered a shameful papist throwback to Old Testament practice.[13] Two years later, John Knox similarly objected to the retention of kneeling for receiving Holy Communion in the 1552 *Book of Common Prayer*. In both cases, Cranmer maintained his position already outlined publicly in the *Book of Common Prayer*. Ceremonies should not "be esteemed equal with God's law," hence, "the keeping or omitting of a

---

[12] Commenting in Latin on a letter of Basil to Gregory the Theologian, *Works in Greek* (Basle: H. Froben, 1532), p. 506 [John Rylands Library, Manchester University, Catalogue Number 18173].

[13] See Diarmaid MacCulloch, *Thomas Cranmer: A Life* (London: Yale University Press, 1996), pp. 471-82; Jennifer Loach, *Edward VI* (New Haven: Yale University Press, 1999), 118-20.

ceremony (in itself considered) is but a small thing: yet the wilful and contemptuous transgression, and breaking of a common order, and discipline, is no small offence before God." Cranmer utterly rejected Knox's argument that "it is not commanded in the Scripture to kneel, and whatsoever is not commanded in the Scripture, is against the Scripture and utterly unlawful and ungodly." Cranmer replied, "This saying is a subversion of all order as well in religion as in common policy."[14]

In the both cases he prevailed. Consequently, when the Articles of Religion first appeared in 1553, they incorporated Cranmer's distinction between matters of salvation and the ordering of the church's common life. On the one hand, as we have seen, Article 20 (of the later Thirty-Nine Articles) stipulated that the church was "a witness and keeper of Holy Writ." Consequently, "it ought not to decree anything against the [Scriptures], so besides the same, ought it not to enforce anything to be believed for necessity of salvation." On the other hand, Article 34 stated that every national church had the right to "ordain, change, and abolish" ecclesiastical ceremonies, since such rites are not divinely instituted, but are "ordained only by man's authority."

Consequently, patterns of worship should reflect "the diversity of countries, times, and men's manners" of the human societies in which churches find themselves. "It is not necessary that traditions and ceremonies be in all places one, or utterly alike." The only caveat to a national church's power in the area of liturgy was "so that nothing be ordained against God's Word." Churches could not shape their liturgies so as to obscure the message of the Gospel they should be proclaiming. In short, according to the historic Anglican formularies, the essentials of salvation, that is, matters of faith and morals, had to be founded on divine authority and, therefore, on the Word of God alone – nothing in addition to it and nothing contrary to it.

Rites and ceremonies, however, as particular expressions of the Gospel for different eras and cultures, were derived from the institutional authority of the church. They must merely not contradict Scripture. The church could use other sources, like ancient tradition, or it could institute new liturgies more in keeping with contemporary

---

[14] MacCulloch, *Cranmer*, p 525-8; Bernard J. Verkamp *The Indifferent Mean: Adiaphorism in the English Reformation to 1554* (Athens, Ohio and Detroit, Michigan: Ohio University and Wayne State University Presses, 1977) pp 63, 67.

needs, even if such practices are not explicitly detailed in Scripture. Thus, the formularies, like Cranmer their chief architect, held that Scripture was the rule for the essentials of faith and morals, but not the blueprint for everything else in life, not even for all matters of church practice, let alone for human society in general.

Here is the origin of the constant refrain in the *Book of Homilies*, the *Book of Common Prayer* and the Thirty-Nine Articles that the Bible contained all things necessary for *salvation*. Here is the crux of Richard Hooker's dispute with those Church of England Puritans who were agitating for changes in the Elizabethan Settlement. Here is the prescient principle that enabled the English national church, with its own rich cultural heritage and history of specific insights into the apostolic faith, to evolve into a truly worldwide Communion that seeks to proclaim a common gospel through a myriad of culturally appropriate prayer books and practices.

Interpreting the Bible.

Alright, we have seen that Cranmer learned from the Fathers the very important point that the Bible was regulative in matters of salvation but not in ordering the life of the church. How should one read Scripture for that saving truth? By insisting on Scripture as the ultimate interpreter of Scripture, of course. That's why the sixteenth-century Anglican triad began with Scripture. Remember we said yesterday that the Article 20 refers to the church as a "keeper" of Scripture in the sense that it is its duty to protect Scripture's role in interpreting itself. But where did Cranmer learn that principle of *sola Scriptura*? Of course, the Bible teaches the unique power of God's Word. Consider Isaiah 55:11, "So is my word that goes out from my mouth: It will not return to me empty, but will accomplish what I desire and achieve the purpose for which I sent it." Cranmer crafts one of his petitions for priests during their ordination accordingly: "Most merciful Father, we beseech thee so to send upon these thy servants thy heavenly blessing . . . that thy word spoken by their mouths may have such success, that it may never be spoken in vain."

Yet, the Fathers read their Bibles, and Cranmer read the Fathers, too. What did he learn from the first commentators on Scripture? For the principles of exegesis, Cranmer looked to Augustine and learned what became known as the commonplace method. According to this approach, the interpreter collects all the Scriptural passages on a given topic in one place (hence the name, common-place), so more difficult passages could be in read in a broader Scripture context to ascertain its meaning. Cranmer quotes Augustine specifically on this method in his "Homily on Salvation." Yet, even after employing the *loci communes* method, not all things associated with the Christian life were clear. Then the Fathers needed to be read as guide to right construal of Scripture.

Cranmer was clear that the Fathers' authority rested on the quality of their biblical exegesis, not on an inspiration equivalent to the apostles, and therefore was variable. Yet, sixteenth-century commentators were no more privileged in their exegetical endeavours. Therefore, even though in Cranmer's view there was no authoritative Patristic consensus beyond what Scripture could clearly support, i.e., the Creeds and the first four councils, no sixteenth-century biblical interpretation was valid unless one could show that it was not unique, that there was Patristic precedence that others had come to the same conclusion based on Scripture.

On this basis, he condemned Luther and Melanchthon's lame Scriptural defence of Philip of Hesse's bigamy as a pastoral remedy in keeping with the Gospel. For Cranmer the fact that such a marriage was literally unprecedented in the whole history of the Christian church rendered such exegesis patently fraudulent. Cranmer would go to great lengths to consult patristic precedent on the matter of the Eucharist in both the 1530s and 1540s, although to opposite conclusions.

Now let's think about what we have said. Anglican biblical commentators are first to compare biblical passages to one another and then their theological conclusions from such activity to the conclusions of earlier generations. That's a lot of comparing. And by the very nature of making a comparison, reason is involved in the process. Hence, as Hooker himself said, the third part of the Anglican triad is not autonomous reason in some post-Enlightenment sense, but rather "theological reasoning," derived from comparing sacred texts to each other and their interpretation by other faithful commentators. Moreover, if the Bible is only regulative in matters of faith and morals, but not in church government or worship, then the church must use prayerful theological reason, derived from the guidance of Scripture and tradition, to make decisions as to how to proclaim the eternal Gospel faithfully to specific cultures and eras. In short, reason was originally part of Anglican theological authority because grace-filled reason was an integral tool in the patristic process of interpretation and application.

Let me now close this point with one more important patristic biblical hermeneutical principle followed by the English Reformers, namely the context in which the Bible was to be read. From the Fathers Cranmer did not learn a hermeneutic of suspicion which characterizes so much of the approach of modern biblical criticism (note the very name!). Rather, Scripture was to be read devotionally. As Cranmer noted again in his copy of Basil's works, "prayer follows from reading."[15] Naturally, Cranmer thought such should be the case for individual study. However, he recognized the best place for a devotional reading of Scripture was in the midst of the community gathered together for corporate worship. Taking to heart a principle he learned from Basil's *Hexameron*, Cranmer decided to make sacred assemblies the place where the average person could learn his Bible. Surely it is not without significance that Cranmer noted in the margin that it was Basil's practice to give daily bible teaching for common labourers in both morning and evening assemblies.[16] Here, rather than monasticism, would seem to be the origin of our daily offices.

Sola gratia.

It's important we understand the difference between unconditional affirmation and unconditional love. Unconditional affirmation is what your dog gives you. He never challenges your right to be the centre of your own universe. Love is not like that. Love by its very nature seeks a relationship, a union, with the beloved. And to enter into relationship the beloved has to give up a measure of autonomy to do so. Naturally, perfect unconditional love seeks to woo and draw out of the beloved an equally selfless, fully giving love in return. The English Reformers believed that the divine grace expressed itself in unconditional love which then sought to draw out a reciprocal love from the beloved. As we said yesterday, this was the whole point of telling the old, old story, to help humanity overcome its spiritual Alzheimer's and find their true fulfilment in God's embrace. For as the living mind of Christ, the Scriptures were the true spiritual DNA of humanity that needed to be reinserted into our minds and hearts so that our wills would be healed and we could respond more properly to God.

In this, Cranmer was also influenced by his reading of the Fathers. For they taught him that the purpose of Scripture was personal and society transformation through redirecting the human heart to truly love God and neighbour. In another comment on Basil's writings

---

[15] Cranmer commenting on Basil's *Works*, p. 506.
[16] Cranmer commenting on Basil's *Works*, p. 18.

perhaps as early as 1532, Cranmer says that when it is imperative for a person to understand himself, he must devote himself to Scripture.[17] In his private theological notebooks around 1538, Cranmer wrote:

> All Scripture is divinely inspired, etc. This text Saint John Chrysostom, Theophilactus, Thomas, with many other authors, both old and new, do expound plainly as the words be that whatsoever truth is necessary to be taught for our salvation, or the contrary to be reproved, whatsoever is necessary for us to do, and what to forbear and not to do, all is completely contained in the Scripture, so that a man thereby may be perfectly instructed unto all manner of goodness.[18]

Not surprisingly, the quotation from Chrysostom made its way into the "Homily on Salvation" along with a reference to Augustine that said that all people are to be 'amended' by Scripture.

Therefore, for Cranmer **sola fide** – justification by faith – did not mean the real absence of an internal change within the individual. No, for Cranmer solifidianism could not mean a real absence of fruitful living. How could it? The Bible plainly calls a Christian to a holy life. Rather the whole point of justification by faith was to make clear the unconditional nature of God's love, for only that would be able to allure a self-centred humanity to love God in return. "Allure"—that's a favourite term of the English reformers for how God's love brought people to saving truth. Here is Cranmer's understanding of the power of God's unconditional love made known in the good news of justification by faith:

> But if the profession of our faith of the remission of our own sins enter within us into the deepness of our hearts, then it must kindle a warm fire of love in our hearts towards God, and towards all other for the love of God – a fervent mind to seek and procure God's honour, will, and pleasure in all things – a good will and mind to help every man and to do good unto them, so far as our might, wisdom, learning, counsel, health, strength, and all other gifts which we have received of God and will extend, – and, *in summa*, a firm intent and purpose to do all

---

[17] Cranmer commenting on Basil's *Works*, p. 79.
[18] British Library Royal MS 7.B.XI, fol. 46r (spelling modernized).

that is good, and leave all that is evil.[19]

In short, for Cranmer, grace produces assurance. Assurance produces gratitude. Gratitude produces love. Love produces repentance. Repentance produces good works. Good works produce a better society. True to the patristic emphasis on transformation, Cranmer taught justification by faith as the only way to bring it about.

To sum up, then, the mind of the English Reformers, they were clearly Bible people, not only because they read the Bible for themselves but also because they were following the example of the Fathers. Only when we understand this can we begin to make sense of the apologetics of John Jewel and Richard Hooker.

7.3. Part Three: The Apologists—Jewel and Hooker

John Jewel (1522–1571) was a Marian exile who ended his life as Bishop of Salisbury. In the light of Pope Pius IV's call for a third session of the Council of Trent, Jewel wrote his famous *Apology of the Church of England* in 1562. In the light of England's recent return to Protestant teaching under the Elizabethan Settlement of 1559, Jewel's *Apology* argued that only by breaking from the Church of Rome and its false teachings could the Church of England stand in the true on-going stream of the church catholic. Not surprisingly, Jewel's key argument was that the medieval innovations of the Roman church had departed from the primitive church and the Fathers, to which the English Reformers had merely returned. The Church of England, not Rome, was faithful to the ancient catholic church. Let me quote a few excerpts from Chapter 5 of the *Apology* to give you a sense of his argument:

> But here I look they will say, though they have not the Scriptures, yet may chance they have the ancient doctors and the holy fathers with them. For this is a high brag they have ever made, how that all antiquity and a continual consent of all ages doth make on their side; and that all our cases be but new, and yesterday's work, and until these few late years were never heard of. Questionless, there can nothing be more spitefully spoken against the religion of God than to accuse it of novelty, as a new come up matter. For as there can be no change in God Himself,

---

[19] J.E. Cox, *Miscellaneous Writings of Thomas Cranmer* (Cambridge: Parker Society, 1846), p. 86.

so ought there to be no change in His religion. Full well know they that nothing is more in the people's favour, or better liketh the common sort, than [the names of Augustine, Jerome, Chrysostom, the Apostles and Christ Himself]. But how if the things, which these men are so desirous to have seem new, be found of greatest antiquity? Contrariwise, how if all the things well-nigh which they so greatly set out with the name of antiquity, having been well and thoroughly examined, be at length found to be but new, and devised of very late?

And as for their religion, if it be of so long continuance as they would have men [believe] it is, why do they not prove it so by the examples of the primitive Church, and by the fathers and councils of old times? Why lieth so ancient a cause thus long in the dust destitute of an advocate? Fire and sword they have had always ready at hand, but as for the old councils and the fathers, all mum--not a word. They did surely against all reason to begin first with these so bloody and extreme means, if they could have found other more easy and gentle ways. And if they trust so fully to antiquity, and use no dissimulation, why did John Clement, a countryman of ours, but few years past, in the presence of certain honest men and of good credit, tear and cast into the fire certain leaves of Theodoret – the most ancient father and a Greek bishop – wherein he plainly and evidently taught that the nature of bread in the Communion was not changed, abolished, or brought to nothing? And this did he of purpose, because he thought there was no other copy thereof to be found. Why saith Albertus Pighius that the ancient father Augustine had a wrong opinion of original sin? and that he erred and lied and used false logic, as touching the case of matrimony concluded after a vow made, which Augustine affirmeth to be perfect matrimony, indeed, and cannot be undone again? Also when they did of late put in print the ancient father Origen's work upon the Gospel of John, why left they quite out the whole sixth chapter?

Wherein it is likely, yea, rather, of very surety, that the said Origen had written many things concerning the sacrament of the Holy Communion contrary to these men's minds; and would put forth that book mangled rather than full and perfect, for fear it should reprove them and their partners of their error. Call ye this trusting to antiquity, when ye rent in pieces, keep back, maim, and burn the ancient fathers' works?

The old fathers Origen and Chrysostom exhort the people to read the Scriptures, to buy them books, to reason at home betwixt themselves of divine matters – wives with their husbands, and parents with their children. These men condemn the Scriptures as dead elements, and – as much as ever they may – bar the people from them.

Hooker

As a first generation reformer, Jewel's major preoccupation was identifying which visible church, England or Rome, was the true catholic church on Earth. Richard Hooker (1554-1600) was a generation later. He was not yet five when Elizabeth came to the throne, and he died while she was still queen. He had only really known a Protestant English culture. If his predecessors had made the case for the distinction between the visible and the invisible, Hooker had a different, double task.

An English Church.

On the one hand he had to explain why the visible church should have an "English face" to quote the Coxians in the famous Frankfurt liturgical fight among the Marian exiles, rather than a purely "Scriptural face." It seemed an obvious historical fact to Hooker that the visible church, as a human institution rooted in contemporary society, had with sound reason adapted its practices to succeeding cultural changes through the centuries.

> But seeing those rites and orders may be at one time more, which at another are less available unto that purpose: what reason is there in these things to urge the state of one only age, as a pattern for all to follow? It is not, I am right sure, their meaning, that we should now assemble our people to serve God in close and secret meetings, or that common brooks and rivers should be used for places of baptism, or that the Eucharist should be ministered after meat, or that the custom of Church feasting should be renewed, or that all kind of standing provision for the ministry should be utterly taken away, and their estate made again dependent upon the voluntary devotion of men. In these things they easily perceive how unfit that were for the present, which was for the first age convenient enough. (*Laws* IV.2.3).

True to Cranmer and Article 34, Hooker maintained the distinction between the unchanging doctrine of the salvation revealed in Scripture and the need to adapt its proclamation to a variety of human societies across space and time.

Yesterday we spoke about Hooker's need to defend Article 34 against the hotter sort of Puritan. For there were indeed those Puritans who conformed to the established church, such as Richard Sibbes and William Perkins. These Puritans concentrated on the reforming human souls until God's grace provided a better day when a monarch would arise in England who would permit further reform of the church. However, as for those who advocated a Presbyterian church government, rather than the historic episcopate, Hooker argued that polity, like liturgy, was a thing indifferent and, thus, able to be left up to the theological reasoning of the local church authorities.

> Neither can I find that men of soundest judgement have otherwise taught, then that articles of belief, and things which all men must of necessity do to the end that they may be saved, are either expressly set down in Scripture, or else plainly thereby to be gathered. But touching things which belong to discipline and outward polity, the Church hath authority to make canons, laws, and decrees, even as we read that in the Apostles times it did. Which kind of laws (for as much as they are not in themselves necessary to salvation) may after they are made be also changed as the difference of times or place shall require. (*Laws* III.10.7)

While Hooker accepted the apostolic foundation of the episcopate, just like the customs of secret meetings and agape feasts which have passed way, for Hooker, apostolic practice (as opposed to apostolic doctrine) did not necessarily mean permanently binding for all time.

What then was the decisive factor in the retention or abolition of an apostolic practice? Effectiveness in proclamation of the Gospel. Mission determined order. As Cranmer had already made clear in the Prayer Book, Hooker argued that the burden of proof was on those who wished to change inherited forms to show how what had been received hindered the Gospel. In the case of England, that meant the retention of the historic three-fold orders, since as we have seen, Cranmer's *Ordinal* presented an episcopate dedicated to proclaiming the Gospel in Word and Sacrament as teachers and pastors of their flock. In short, to use the technical theological language, Hooker argued that the historic succession of three-fold orders was in England of the *bene esse* of the church (the well ordering of it) rather than of the *esse* of the church (its essential nature). In less exalted language, an English church with historic orders was simply the best possible boat from which to fish.

The Mystical Church.

Nevertheless, for Hooker's era, it was not enough to concentrate on the visible church as distinct from the invisible church. He was equally concerned to show how the visible church, as a human institution thoroughly rooted in each nation's culture, would still fulfil its divine vocation ultimately at the end of the age by becoming one with invisible church. Therefore, he wanted to stress not the difference between but rather the inherent connection of the visible and invisible church.

Hooker's very sophisticated understanding of the church is but an expression of his overall sacramental world view that God is working through all creation by his laws to reconcile it to himself. God works through finite things to bring them back into relation with the infinite. However, for convenience sake, let's just look at one aspect of Hooker's thought in this area. Human salvation. If one could say that Rome viewed the institutional church like Christ, both human and divine, but without error, Hooker viewed the institutional church as an example of his redemptive activity, thoroughly human in a post-lapsidarian sense, but an object of grace, divinely called for eventual reunion with God, but by three distinct steps: justification, sanctification, and glorification:

> There is a glorifyinge righteousness of men in the Worlde to comme, and there is a justifying and sanctifying righteousness here. The righteousness wherewith we shalbe clothed in the world to comme, is both perfect and inherente: that whereby here we are justified is perfecte but not inherente, that whereby we are sanctified, inherent but not perfecte. (Just. 3)

Justification was by imputation through faith alone. Sanctification was the result of receiving the Spirit of Adoption in the heart which infused virtues which then bring forth 'the fruites, the workes, the operacions of the spirit' (*ibid*). Although Hooker consistently stressed faith as the formal cause of justification, he stressed even more the importance of the habitual righteousness of sanctification that necessarily accompanied it.

Where then did sinners encounter the Spirit of God which made participation in him possible? Hooker was quite clear – the church. This was not a denial of the Protestant principle that faith came by hearing the Word of God preached, but once again putting that principle in a wider theological context of divine law. As God made Eve from the rib of

Adam, so God made the church out of Christ's wounded and bleeding side (*Laws* V.56.7). Salvation comes by participation in Christ through the divinely appointed means of his church. God as primary cause made the Church out of Christ, the secondary cause, who works to reconcile God and humanity by his sacrifice.

How does supernatural birth take place in the church? Through the traditional Anglican understanding of Word and Sacraments as divine instruments for administering the Spirit. Let's look more carefully at each one.

1) **Word**. Although usually overlooked, Hooker was just as insistent as Cranmer that the Word was an instrument of the Holy Spirit. He fiercely objected to the Puritan dislike of the "bare reading of the word of God" in the daily offices, because "they mightily strive to obscure" how "his gracious Spirit" is "the principal virtue" in Scripture which there manifests "itself for the endless good of men's souls, even the virtue which it hath to *convert*, to *edify*, to *save* souls." Although the Puritans stressed the importance of the exposition of Scripture for bringing people to salvation, Hooker accused them of appropriating the saving power of the Holy Spirit to themselves, rather than to the Scriptures. (*Laws* V.22.1). According to Hooker, "surely the power of the word of God, even without the help of interpreters in Gods Church worketh mightily, not unto their confirmation alone which are converted, but also to their conversion which are not" (*Laws* V.22.4).

2) **Sacraments**. For Hooker, Baptism and Communion are primarily marks to know when God imparts the grace of participation. As "moral instruments of salvation," they are the ordinary means of grace. In the rite of baptism, God accomplishes "the work of our new birth." Water is the instrument "whereby [grace] is received unto incorporation into Christ," his righteousness is imputed and "the first and most effectual cause out of which our belief growth" is imparted. Through baptism, the person of Christ is wholly present in man. In Communion, we participate in his Spirit-quickened humanity by degrees. Christ is not in the consecrated bread and wine, but they are instruments which are "conducts of life and conveyances of his body and blood" to those who receive with faith. In other words, we receive their effects in us. Thus, the "real presence of Christ's most blessed body and blood is not therefore to be sought for in the sacrament, but in the worthy receiver of the sacrament." (*Laws* V.67.6). Baptism was the sacrament for participation in Christ through justification. Communion was the sacrament for participation in Christ through sanctification. Since the

spiritual effect of Communion was to strengthen a believer's inherent righteousness, Hooker can even speak of the transubstantiation of the recipient rather than of what was received.

Since the human earthly national Church of England was also the divinely appointed means of grace by which God would gather his mystical church, what Hooker said about individual Christians, can be said about his view of the visible church. In this world, because God has established this human institution for his divine purposes,

i) like the justified, it is acceptable to God as his church, and his Spirit works through it, despite its many failings,

ii) yet like those being sanctified, because God's Spirit is at work in the human institutional church, it can reflect his character in a greater or lesser degree, and

iii) like the glorified, one day the various human institutional churches will be purged and merged and become co-terminus with the mystical church. In that moment the church made manifest in the Eucharist will then be manifest for all eternity.

8. The Anglican Mind in Caroline and Tractarian Thought

The Revd Canon Arthur Middleton

8.1. Ressourcement Theology

Let me begin in the mid-twentieth century in France with some French theologians, that included Henri de Lubac, Jean Danélou, Henri Bouillard, Yves Congar, Louis Bouyer and Marie-Dominique Chenu, and the Swiss, von Balthasar. They initiated a remarkable theological movement termed *ressourcement* theology. It was not a unified school of thought but these theologians shared a common belief that the writings of the early church constitute an incomparable source for the contemporary renewal of the Church. Here were sources for a deeper understanding of the gospel in our world and for the renewal of liturgy and the sustaining of our spiritual life. In a post-Christian Europe, these *ressourcement* theologians turned to the work of great patristic and medieval theologians such as Origen, Ignatius of Antioch, Cyprian, Chrysostom, Cyril of Alexandria, Augustine, John of Damascus, and Thomas Aquinas.

Here they recovered crucial sources for the revitalization of contemporary theology and pastoral life. This movement emphasized the central role of the biblical text in theological argument. This emphasis on a return to the sources offered a vision of Catholic theology that differed subtly but radically from what was almost universally available in the textbooks of the time. It was a theology that was deliberately crafted to break out of the clerical, apologetic, largely anti-Protestant and anti-modern forms of thinking that had bound it for a century and more. Their aim was to find in the textual roots of the Christian tradition inspiration for a theology more open to ecumenical dialogue, more engaged with the social needs of the modern world and more nourishing for the spiritual hunger of lay people. Chenu, a French Dominican, argued that theology is not simply reasoning about the church's official teachings, but that it expresses the mind's serious engagement with its own conversion to God through Christ Jesus. Therefore theology is always radically historical in its way of reasoning, simply because God has revealed himself to human beings in the contingent events and characters of history.

> To see the world from a particular standpoint which our tradition has given us is the condition of creaturely knowledge. To trust a tradition for the insight and knowledge it has given us, to go on to appropriate more of what it has to offer, is not irrational, nor is it necessarily conservative. Even the revolutionary, whatever his destination, can see only from where he is.[1]

What we have in the resources of the patristic tradition that has been appropriated into Anglicanism by the Reformers, the Carolines, the Tractarians and others, is a tradition that was outside the parameters of their particular time and thought, the solitary confinement of the 'present'. It offered to them alternatives that were not available to the historically-limited world of their time and enabled them to escape from the imprisoning effects of their contemporary religious controversies by bringing a productive past that still lived in the Church. It brought a critical stance to those controversies of their time and enabled them to render the more recent answers of their time questionable and not to be accepted simply as given. The appropriation of the patristic mind, this way of doing theology, enhanced the life of Anglicanism beyond the increasingly closed options of the sixteenth, seventeenth and nineteenth centuries. This was by no means regression into conservatism, a simple conservation of the past. These theologians were concerned with the future, to find in the past the way into the future by reading and listening attentively to the Fathers in order to find where they dissented from the Reformation controversies, and what they offered as constructive solutions, for therein may lie their relevance.

What results, particularly so in the Carolines and the Tractarians, is a contextualization of the patristic mind within the parameters of an English theology, as they used the thought and piety of the Fathers within the structure of their own theological vision. This brought the resources of the past into a positive and critical relationship with their own particular historical context for the sake of the future, but allowed that historical context to be critical of these same resources from the past. In their *return to the Fathers,* they demonstrated how the theology of their day could overcome its inner weakness and

---

[1] R. J. Bauckham, 'Tradition in relation to Scripture and Reason' in *Scripture, Tradition and Reason, A Study in the Criteria of Christian Doctrine,* eds. B. Drewery and R. J Buckham (T. & T. Clark, Edinburgh, 1988), p. 133.

deficiencies. This was not done by a mere repetition of the Fathers or the transforming of them into a purely formal and infallible authority, and their theology into a patristic scholasticism. What we find in this Anglican appropriation is the recovery of the spirit of the Fathers, of the secret inspiration that made them true witnesses of the Church and the acquiring of their mind. They recovered and made their own the experience of the Church not as mere 'Institution, doctrine or system', but as the all-transforming *life,* the passage into the reality of redemption and transfiguration.

They saw that you cannot enter into the truth of Christianity apart from its history, and that the historical *condition* of Christian truth is not something that starts in Bethlehem and ends on Calvary. It applies equally to the Church, the Body of Christ. It placed them in the larger room of the Christian centuries and freed them from the solitary confinement of the present. As masters of English theology they represent the new point of departure, from which the Church of England started on her career as a Reformed Branch of the ancient Catholic Church.

In doing this they avoided the defect of so much theology today, the division between theology and spirituality. It is a dissociation between the mind and the heart, between thought and feeling, that has its roots in what T. S. Eliot described as 'a dissociation of sensibility', and is damaging to theology, threatening its fabric in both its spiritual and intellectual aspects. Cut off from the movement of the heart towards God, theology finds itself in a void. Being steeped in patristic divinity, our divines avoided this contemporary phenomenon of a dissociation between thought and feeling. To repeat the characteristic phrase of Michael Ramsey they 'did their theology to the sound of church bells' because they understood the issue of theology to be, 'not only one of intellectual clarity but of a union of human lives with God in the way of holiness'.

It was in the many-sided thought and sanctified divinity of the undivided Church that they found a theology that knew of no such dissociation between thought and feeling, between theology and spirituality. There they discovered that *theologia,* in its strictest sense is discourse about God, in his being and relations, the doctrine of the Trinity. In a wider sense it means also contemplation of the Trinity, because, as Evagrius claimed, the one who prays is a theologian and the theologian is one who prays, or in the words of John Klimakos, 'the climax of purity is the beginning of theology'. The theologian lives in the

Trinity. For '*theologia* is the apprehension of God by a man restored to the image and likeness of God, and within this apprehension there can be discovered two sides, what *we* call the intellectual and the affective'.[2]

8.2. *Ancient Faith for the Church's Future*

Ancient Faith for the Church's Future[3] is a significant book of essays written by Anglican Evangelicals and Roman Catholics. The essays from the Wheaton Theology Conference 2007 set out to demonstrate the lively and significant importance of the patristic mind for contemporary Christian witness and practice. The concern is to engage with the witness of Christians throughout the history of the church which has been inspired by God's Word.

> When the content of the church's confession coheres with the witness of Scripture, and when Scripture is regarded as the ground of the church's tradition, respect for the place of tradition is a matter of considerable importance ... when a given tradition is consonant with God's self-revelation, it is to be upheld and honoured by the Church. On this count, the early confessions, creeds, hymns, commentaries, sermons and works of theology constitute a deposit or treasury of ancient witnesses.[4]

The inspiration came from an earlier call in 2006 in the document *A Call to an Ancient Evangelical Future*, by Robert Webber and Phil Kenyon. It is a call to examine our faithfulness to God's revelation in Jesus Christ, authoritatively recorded in Scripture and handed down through the Church. The *Introduction* continues with a call for

> the Church's reflection to remain anchored in the Scriptures in continuity with the theological interpretation learned from the early Fathers. Thus, the call to Evangelicals is to turn away from methods that separate theological reflection from the common traditions of the Church.[5]

---

[2] Andrew Louth, *Discovering the Mystery: An Essay on the Nature of Theology* (Oxford, Clarendon, 1983) p 3.
[3] *Ancient Faith for the Church's Future* ed. Mark Husbands and Jeffrey P. Greenman (Nottingham, IVP Academic 2008)
[4] Introduction, *Ancient Faith for the Church's Future*, p. 9.
[5] Introduction, *Ancient Faith for the Church's Future*, p 9.

Anti-historical attitudes also disregard the common biblical and theological legacy of the ancient Church. This Call stands in a much larger tradition, to learn from one of the most significant theological developments of the twentieth century, *ressourcement* theology as previously referred to.

C. S. Lewis, using the analogy of conversation, says that coming late to a discussion results in missing the drift of what is being said because of being absent from the conversation's early stages. So in thinking about faith 'the only safety is to have a standard of plain, central Christianity which puts the controversies of the moment in their proper perspective. Such a standard can be acquired only from the old books.'[6] 'With a sense of the long theological tradition, the reader has a chance, at least, of seeing beyond the real and tragic present divisions and confusions within the Christian family to "something positive, self-consistent, and inexhaustible," running through every age, something that expresses for us a still more fundamental unity in faith and moral vision.'[7] In conversation with Irenaeus, Origen and Augustine, it is only within a 'worshiping, discerning, interpreting, preaching church that Scripture becomes Scripture – is received as a canon and generates the rule of faith.'[8]

8.3. Caroline Ressourcement

The "great figures", the Caroline Divines, the successors of the Reformers, were builders, their work being the natural outcome and growth of what the Reformers had laid, not merely in the opinions of thinkers but in the foundation documents of Anglicanism. If those foundations had not been there Anglican theology in the seventeenth century would have been quite different.

These Anglican divines of the seventeenth century continue to hold the Fathers in special esteem, but as Michael Ramsey pointed out:

> Whereas the Edwardian and Elizabethan divines had been interested in the Fathers chiefly as a means of proving what had or had not been the primitive doctrine and practice, the Caroline

---

[6] C. S. Lewis, 'An Introduction', in *St Athanasius on the Incarnation*, translated and edited by A Religious of CSMV (A. R. Mowbray, 1963) pp. 3ff..

[7] Old Books and Contemporary Faith, The Bible, Tradition and the Renewal of Theology, Brian E. Daley, S.J. in in *Ancient Faith for the Church's Future*, p 54.

[8] *Old Books and Contemporary Faith*, p66

divines went farther in using the thought and piety of the Fathers within the structure of their own theological exposition. Their use of the Fathers had these two noteworthy characteristics.

(1) Not having, as did the Continental Reformers, a preoccupation with the doctrines of justification or predestination they followed the Fathers of the Nicene age in treating the Incarnation as the central doctrine of the faith. Indeed a feeling of the centrality of the Incarnation became a recurring feature of Anglican divinity, albeit the Incarnation was seen as S. Athanasius saw it in its deeply redemptive aspect.

(2) Finding amongst the Fathers the contrast of Greek and Latin divinity, the Anglican divines could be saved from western narrowness, and were conscious that just as the ancient undivided Church embraced both East and West so too the contemporary Catholic Church was incomplete without the little known Orthodox Church of the East as well as the Church in the West, Latin, Anglican and Reformed. The study of the Fathers created the desire to reach out to Eastern Christendom. Thus did Anglican theology find in the study of the Fathers first a gateway to the knowledge of what was scriptural and primitive, subsequently a living tradition which guided the interpretation of Scripture, and finally a clue to the Catholic Church of the past and the future: in the words of Lancelot Andrewes 'the whole Church Catholic, Eastern, Western, our own.'[9]

It is not surprising that no period in our Church's history is richer in writers of high distinction in the field of theology, a feature which did not diminish until the end of the century in an age of general intellectual ferment. These distinguished writers include Hooker and Andrewes, Laud, Hammond and Thorndike, Overall, Field, Ussher, Sanderson, Taylor, Pearson, Barrow and Bull, to name but a few. Walter Frere of the Community of the Resurrection, claimed that with Hooker, Andrewes and Overall there came a revulsion against the dominant Calvinism,

> which introduced a more mature conception of the position of the English Church, based upon the appeal to Scripture and the principles of the undivided Church. The earlier theologians had

---

[9] A. M. Ramsey, "The Ancient Fathers and Modern Anglican Theology", *Sobornost*, Series 4:6 Winter-Spring 1962.

been able to recognize in principle the soundness of this appeal, but they had hitherto been unable to work out in practice its detailed results.[10]

If one was to define the ethos of these Caroline divines then it will be found in the holding together of what Baron von Hügel maintained as necessary strands of the Christian life, the mystical, the intellectual and the institutional.

> It was marked by a time of massive scholarly activity. Following on the classical work of Richard Hooker (1554-1600) which only began to be assimilated in the years following his death, it saw the beginnings of a distinctively Anglican theological position, on the one side clearly distinguished from Rome, on the other from that of Calvinist Geneva. Above all it was marked by a renewal of the understanding and the practice of the Christian way of common and private prayer. And all these things were held together in a single focus.[11]

In the theology of these divines thinking and praying are indissolubly connected, in an orthodoxy which was not a static repetition of the past but a living, growing pattern of truth.

> Prof. Owen Chadwick wrote,

> ... if High Churchmen of that age like Bramhall or Thorndike had been asked what led them not to compromise, they would have replied in terms like the following: Our paramount duty is to the Catholic Church; our subordinate and derivative duty is to the Church of England as the representative of the Catholic Church in this country. The Catholic Church is known by its faithfulness to the primitive model. The Church of England has no choice but to follow that model, must seek to apply the principle rigorously and exactly. "I am satisfied", wrote Thorndike in 1660, "that the differences, upon which we are divided, cannot be justly settled upon any terms, which any part of the *Whole* Church shall have just cause to refuse, as inconsistent with the unity of the *Whole* Church.

Chadwick continued,

---

[10]   W.H.Frere, *A History of the English Church in the Reigns of Elizabeth and James I 1558 - 1625* (London, 1904), p 284.

[11]   A. M. Allchin, *The Dynamic of Tradition* (London, DLT, 1981), p 56.

The argument ... represents a contention which has survived the centuries and must still be reckoned with ... Any act which divides Anglicanism from the universal Church of the centuries is to be rejected, even if that act offers temporary or local advantage; and the test of universality, in this sad, divided state of Christendom, may be found in appeal to the ancient and undivided Church of the first centuries. The question whether there are sufficient ambiguities or exceptions in the Episcopal practice of the ancient Church to warrant modern exceptions, Thorndike answered with a vigorous 'no'.[12]

What he is saying is that the Primitive model of the undivided Church must be the interpretative principle of Anglicanism because it transcends party labels.

8.4. Tractarian Ressourcement

In principle this is what the Tractarians were doing for the revitalization of the Church of England in the nineteenth century. Their *ressourcement* theology was Caroline divinity which led them to patristic sources. Their concern was to focus on the doctrine and discipline of the One, Holy Catholic and Apostolic Church and so they turned not only to these same patristic theologians but also to those seventeenth century theologians whose classical Anglican mind had been formed by them. Here they found that our reading of the Bible should be mediated not primarily through the secondary sources of post-Reformation manuals – what C. S. Lewis would label "new books" – but through the "old books" of the Fathers of the Church, who were the first to recognize and receive the Christian biblical canon, which is the spirit of the English Reformers.

Michael Ramsey claimed that next to the Reformers in the sixteenth century and the Caroline divines in the seventeenth century it was the Tractarians who specially cherished the appeal to the ancient Fathers. Divines in England endeavoured to restore a due and proper estimation to the primitive writings: John Kaye (1783-1853), on his election as Regius Professor of Divinity in Cambridge in 1816, became the first to recall theological students to the study of the Fathers. The

---

[12]   Chadwick Preface, *From Uniformity to Unity 1662-1962*, ed. Geoffrey F. Nuttall and Owen Chadwick (London, SPCK, 1962), pp 13, 15-16.

appeal to the Fathers among the Tractarians was a living heritage despite a decline in this among eighteenth century Latitudinarian divines.

So the Tractarian appeal to the ancient Fathers was not the rediscovery that some have tended to assume. There is before them a line of eminent men of learning and what happened in 1833 had been smouldering in what Dean Burgon described, as the 'residuum of the altar-fires of a long succession of holy and earnest men',[13] who were not Tractarians themselves but were the precursors of the Tractarians and it was from these men that they inherited what has been described truly as English Church theology.

The need is to light up those parts of our system, existence of which is not in doubt but which have been thrown into the shade, by pouring in the light of Antiquity. Enable people to study the wholesome tone of doctrine contained in the writings of the great Lights of the Church. In Oxford Dr. Charles Lloyd, the Regius Professor of Divinity, in his lectures on the *Book of Common Prayer* gave quite a new view to many of his hearers, some of whom became prominent in the movement such as Newman, Pusey, Hurrell Froude, Isaac Williams, and Frederick Oakeley. Lloyd's teaching affected the movement deeply. As an independent thinker Lloyd was considerably in advance of the high churchmen of his time. His Lectures on the Prayer Book informed his students of the sources from which all that is best and noblest in the English liturgy is derived. Pusey was a thorough disciple of Dr. Lloyd.

The publication of William Palmer's *Antiquities of the English Ritual with a Dissertation on Primitive Liturgies,* published in 1832, is a chief factor in the preparation for the movement which was fast approaching. Palmer was 'insisting upon the almost forgotten fact that the Prayer Book is mainly a translation from earlier office-books, and so represents the descent of the Reformed Church of England from the church of earlier days, it powerfully contributed to increase that devotion to the traditions of the church which characterised the Tracts.'[14]

Here the Tractarians found that Anglican theological method always included what was mentioned earlier, a concern for church history and the 'proper' historical setting or context of the Bible: that is, the living apostolic community, the catholic Church of the Fathers, which ensures authoritatively, normatively, and critically, the historic continuity of the

[13] J. W. Burgon, *Lives of Twelve Good Men* (London, John Murray, 1891), p 81..

[14] H P Liddon, *Life of Edward Bouverie Pusey in 4 vols* (Longmans, Green & Co London 1893-7) vol. i.p 264.

apostolic community and her apostolic faith and praxis. This ecclesial dimension was appropriated by Anglicanism and made the basis of Christian living, the context of Christian thinking. Studying and preaching Scripture in its context must be the main source of Anglican renewal. This renewal came with the Oxford Movement under the leadership of Keble, Froude, Newman and Pusey, the parish priests, and the rediscovery of the monastic life for men and women.

8.5. Conversation

Here in conversation with these Fathers, Irenaeus, Tertullian, Origen, the Cappadocians, Augustine et al, our Reformers, our Caroline and Tractarian forbears, we will discover how they confronted the revisionists of their day in the Arian and Gnostic ideologies and in their antipathy to the Church's tradition. With their preconceived notions these revisionists assailed the Church's orthodoxy with their own Scriptural hermeneutic that was enslaved to the letter and devoid of an ecclesial sense of living tradition, which, with Scripture comprises a single sacred deposit of the Word of God. Today we need to confront the contemporary revisionists in the Gnostic/Feminist and secularist ideologies attacking the Church's orthodoxy, who have fallen captive to a hermeneutic of sociological reductionism in the political correctness that is more akin to Marx than Augustine and again is devoid of an ecclesial sense of living tradition.

It was the patristic mind that took shape in the Anglican mind of the Reformers and Caroline Divines that was instrumental in the renewal of Anglicanism and the inspiring of the Tractarians. This was their *ressourcement* theology, the theology of the Oxford Movement, and it was ecclesiological. Therefore, to elucidate the principles of Caroline and Tractarian divinity and work for the renewal of the Anglican Communion we will need to re-engage with this *ressourcement* theology.

8.6. Our Battle

Our battle today is against all that would make us captive to a sociological reductionism as the interpretative principle of Anglicanism that uses political correctness to re-interpret the Bible and apostolic faith and order. It is a secularism that stalks the Church and would reduce Christian Faith and Life to a respectable secular humanism. It wants to set the agenda for the Anglican Communion and dresses it in Christian language. It is what I call genetically modified theology and like genetically modified crops we cannot tell where it will lead us as sight is lost of where we have come from. In a time like this it is crucial that we know what the patrimony of Anglicanism is as the great theologians of our Anglican tradition did. This Anglican *ressourcement* has certain distinguishing features:

The Constant

First, its constant is the Catholic faith of the Primitive church, the *faith once for all delivered to the saints,* summarized in the Rule of Faith or Scripture and the Creeds. This is the doctrine of the Anglican Communion and she refuses to affirm as of the faith any doctrine not so qualified in or by Scripture or the Primitive Church. John Jewel affirmed, in his *Apologia,* that "Scripture and the Primitive Church are the criteria by which the authenticity of a Church and the truth of its teaching are assessed"[15] and John Bramhall claimed that the Church of England was not "a new Church, a new Religion, or new Holy Orders."[16] This constant of the Anglican patrimony is found in different shapes from the 16th Century onwards.

Distinctiveness

Secondly, its distinctiveness is derived from theological method, not content, and emerged with Archbishop Parker's theological interpretation of the Elizabethan Settlement in the 1571 Thirty-Nine Articles, *The Second Book of Homilies* and the "Canon of Preaching". Rooted doctrinally in Scripture and antiquity, we find this method in the works of Anglican divines and in our formularies. Richard Hooker articulated it in his *Of the Laws of Ecclesiastical Polity,* and Michael Ramsey describes its spirit as, "... doing theology to the sound of church bells," to stress the essential connection between theology, doctrine and Christian worship. *The Book of Common Prayer* is as much about a way of doing theology as about liturgy, *lex orandi est lex credendi,* which means that the Rule of Prayer governs the Rule of Belief; and as Athanasius's theology cannot be understood apart from the liturgy of Bishop Serapion, so Anglicanism cannot be understood apart from *The Book of Common Prayer.*

For Hooker, God's revelation in Christ and the Church – what is called *the Whole Christ* – is authoritative, but the language in which it is

---

[15]   1562: *Apologia for the Church of England,* John Jewel, Bishop of Salisbury, being the chief author.

[16]   Archbishop John Bramhall *Works,* Vol.I. Library of Anglo-Catholic Theology, p 119. . See http://anglicanhistory.org/lact/

expressed is not infallible. In essence it is rational but mysterious, defying exact definition. Lancelot Andrewes put it succinctly: "One canon ... two testaments, three creeds, four general councils, five centuries and the series of the Fathers in that period ... determine the boundary of our faith".[17]

Divine Revelation

Thirdly, God's revelation does not deny God's presence in creation. C.S.Lewis,[18] whose theology was greatly influenced by Hooker, noted that Hooker's universe was "drenched with Deity" and Hooker's words "All things that are of God, have God in them and they in himself likewise, and yet their substance and his are very different." Lewis spells out what this presence of the transcendent God in his world implies, keeping together things that can easily be set in opposition, reason as well as revelation, nature as well as grace, the commonwealth as well as the Church, are equally though diversely, 'of God ... All kinds of knowledge, all good arts, sciences and disciplines ... we meet in all levels the divine wisdom shining out through 'the beautiful variety of things' in 'their manifold and yet harmonious dissimilitude'.

This is nothing less than the patristic vision of God's creation filled with his energy and wisdom, the presence of God participating in his world which can be the only context within which to speak of man's participation in God in terms of deification. 'The Word of God, who is God, wills in all things and at all times to work the mystery of his embodiment'.[19] Within this context Hooker expounds a vision of man which finds its fulfilment in God, a theocentric humanism. 'If then in him we are blessed, it is by force of participation and conjunction with him ... so that although we be men, yet being into God united we live as it were the life of God'. [20] This divine presence is one in revelation and nature, creation and redemption, consistent and reasonable. In revelation it brings to a climax what God does in nature and in nature it gives us the clue to revelation, because "The Word" that "became flesh" is the Word or *Logos* at work in all creation. So the Incarnation becomes central and primary to Anglican theology. We see

[17] *Opuscula quaedam posthuma*, Lancelot Andrewes, J.H. Parker, 1852 (Library of Anglo-Catholic Theology) p 91.
[18] C. S. Lewis, " English Literature in the Sixteenth Century, excluding drama ", *The Oxford History of English Literature* (Oxford, OUP, 1954), p 460
[19] A. M. Allchin, *The Kingdom of Love and Knowledge* (London, DLT, 1979), Ch 6.
[20] Hooker, *Of The Laws of Ecclesiastical Polity*,Bk. I. xi, 2.

this appreciation of the natural world in those great poets of our Anglican tradition – George Herbert, Henry Vaughan, Thomas Traherne, John Keble, T. S. Eliot and R. S. Thomas.

Scripture, Tradition

Fourthly, Michael Ramsey claimed that it was the nature of Elizabethan theology rather than imitation of Hooker in the style of Lutherans to Luther or Calvinists to Calvin that made it possible to creatively appeal to Scripture and tradition and it must remain so today. Scripture is the supreme authority because it contains all things necessary to salvation, but not as regulations for everything in the Church's life, for the Church has authority to decree rites and ceremonies. Our Formularies affirm the Old Testament revealing Christ by pointing to him and the New Testament revealing Christ fulfilling what is foreshadowed in the Old. The Bible is about God's saving work and self-revelation through law and prophets, Christ being the head and climax. Scripture became the self-evident basis but because the Bible without the Church becomes a mere collection of ancient documents, Scriptural interpretation depends on the appeal to antiquity as mutually inclusive. The Bible and the Church must be dancing partners and where the one is detached from the other it leads to an uncontrollable doctrinal space-flight. Anglicanism maintained the Catholic notion of a perfect union between Scripture and Tradition or the Church and Scripture in that the Church's authority is not distinct from that of Scripture but rather that they are one.

George Tavard, the Jesuit claimed that, in making Scripture the self-evident basis of Anglicanism but alongside Tradition as mutually inclusive, a consistency with the patristic spirit is maintained. Anglican divinity has an ecclesial context in which the Church bears witness to the truth not by reminiscence or from the words of others, but from its own living, unceasing experience, from its Catholic fullness that has its roots in the Primitive Church. This appeal is not merely to history but to a charismatic principle, tradition, which together with Scripture contains the truth of divine revelation, a truth that lives in the Church. In this spirit Anglican divines looked to the Fathers as interpreters of Scripture. The 1571 Canons authorize preachers to preach nothing but what is found in Holy Scripture and what the ancient Fathers have collected from the same, ensuring that the interpretation of Scripture is consistent with what Christians have believed always, everywhere and by all, the Vincentian Canon. The voice of the Bible could be plainly heard only if its texts were interpreted broadly and rationally, in accordance with the apostolic creed and the evidence of the historical practice of Christendom. Only the heretics relied most on isolated texts and ignored scriptural principles.

Reason

Fifthly, Anglican theological method appeals to reason. Hooker's response to Puritan narrowness, which saw the Bible as a handbook of regulations for everything in life and religion, was to elucidate a much wider and realistic understanding of divine law. God is Creator as well as Redeemer. The harmony and purpose in the natural order are expressions of the divine Reason which lies behind Scripture and the decrees of Church Councils, emanating from God himself and found in the lives of all his creatures. God's revelation comes to us in various ways and our reason and conscience arrives at knowledge of God's will by a number of concurrent means and faculties. In creation God reveals himself as the principle of rationality, purpose and unity, described as the divine *Logos* that informs our consciences and minds enabling us to perceive purpose and order in the universe. Such knowledge requires revelation to complete it and redemption to cleanse and free the heart and mind from things that inhibit and corrupt us. It is an appeal within the context of the appeal to Scripture and antiquity. Unbalancing in one direction degenerates into the ghetto mentality of either Scripturalism, or Traditionalism, or Liberalism. The 19th century scientific undermining of Christianity found this threefold appeal able to respond to and absorb scientific method and historical criticism.

The fashionable addition of *experience* is unnecessary because Tradition enfolds past and present, and embraces as its source and power the contemporaneity of the Gospel through which the true character of present experience is refracted and thereby critically evaluated. It is a way of looking at and experiencing the world; but with the kingdom of God, the *sui generis* experience of the Church and not the world as the ultimate term of reference.

Dean Church pointed out that Andrewes recalled an age into a diviner, purer, freer air, back to the many-sided thought, to the sanctified divinity of the undivided Church. By the influence of this divinity he led his contemporaries away from a theology which ended in cross-grained and perverse conscientiousness to a theology which ended in adoration, self-surrender and blessing, and in the awe and joy of welcoming the Eternal Beauty, the Eternal Sanctity and the Eternal Love, the Sacrifice and Reconciliation of the world.[21] This fusion of thought and feeling in Hooker and Andrewes is what drew that 20th century man of letters, T.S.Eliot, back to Christian faith and life and prompted his small book of essays *For Lancelot Andrewes,* who for Eliot embodied in himself the learning, the theology and the devotion which marks the best men of this age. For Eliot, Hooker and Andrewes made the English Church more worthy of intellectual assent, and in them, as in the actual life and worship of the period, he found a Catholicism which was not ignorant either of the Renaissance or the Reformation. Here for Eliot was a tradition which had already moved into the modern world that was a way of living and thinking the Christian tradition and which had taken humanism and criticism into itself, without being destroyed by them.

8.7. A Postscript

Let me end with a postscript concerning Catholics and Evangelicals.

The Evangelical Revival and the Oxford Movement have been two great post-Reformation movements of revival in the Anglican Church that gave their respective shape to the two principal traditions, the Evangelical and the Catholic, which today exist side by side and with great vigour in our Church. Both traditions are older than these revivals. Their continuity and homogeneous development can be traced from Reformation times: through Nicholas Ridley, bishop of London, to Charles Simeon (1759-1836); through Lancelot Andrewes, bishop of Winchester, to Bishop Charles Gore (1853-1932); through Nicholas Ferrar of Little Gidding to Richard Meux Benson, the founder of the Society of St John the Evangelist at Cowley (1824-1915). At all periods throughout these centuries, we observe men of great piety and devotion within both traditions:

> Henry Martyn, the Evangelical missionary (1781-1812) and John Keble, one of the fathers of the Oxford Movement (1792-1866); Charles Simeon, one of the main leaders of the Evangelical Revival and Edward Bouverie Pusey, the outstanding Tractarian leader (1800-82); James Hannington, the Evangelical bishop of East Equatorial Africa (1847-85) and Frank Weston, the Anglo-Catholic bishop of Zanzibar(1871-1924). Yet the differences between each pair of men seem to disappear, when contrasted

---

[21]   R. Church, "Lancelot Andrewes" in *Masters of English Theology,* ed. A. Barry (London, 1877), p 90.

with the Christ-centred devotion which enlivened them all ... The remarkable feature of the different types of devotion, shown by various saintly men of the Church of England, is not the tenacity with which each holds to his particular tradition, but their common devotion to Christ. This devotion has always grown, and still grows, out of the love and study of the Scriptures, and out of an affectionate adherence to the piety of the *Book of Common Prayer*. Neither the Catholic nor the Evangelical type of Anglican holiness can be explained in terms of a practical *via media,* or of a Church which is committed to some form of Anglo-Saxon compromise."[22]

Such men like Henry Venn and Charles Simeon were not only Evangelicals but Churchmen because while they emphasized personal experience and commitment to Christ they held the doctrines contained in the Articles, Prayer Book and Homilies. I would describe these as classical Anglican Evangelicals in their commitment to an emphasis on personal experience of Christ and their adherence to the ecclesiology of the *Book of Common Prayer* that is often lacking in some Evangelicals today. The emphasis of many Evangelicals today is on Gospel ministry and preaching is exalted above Sacraments – reducing salvation to *gnosis,* knowledge, rather than grace, that Hooker condemned as Gnostic heresy. Sir Edwyn Hoskyns would always remind Evangelicals that the Gospel implied the Church. The fruits of Evangelical revival enriched the Oxford Movement when heirs from Evangelical homes became leading Tractarians. To quote again the Belgian Benedictine turned Anglican, de Mendieta, The fullness of Anglicanism will be utterly catholic and uncompromisingly evangelical at the same time".[23] Both these emphases are present in the New Testament making it necessary to set such Scriptural truths and realities in their Scriptural complementarity. Michael Ramsey claimed that the Anglican Church does not see the Evangelical and the Catholic views as alternatives, but in the Scriptural sense where both elements are one. This ethos has enabled the Anglican Communion to look not for a synthesis but rather for a symbiosis, a growing together in a living whole of the sundered Christian traditions and with humility seek to promote it. They can do so because in its own ecclesial life the Anglican Communion has found these evangelical and catholic elements to be complementary and necessary to the fullness of a Church's life and mission.

---

[22] Emmanuel Amand de Mendieta, *Anglican Vision,* (London, SPCK, 1971.), p 38
[23] de Mendieta, *Ibid.*pg 38

9. Anglican Ecclesiology: Summary of its History and Current Assessment

The Revd Dr Ashley Null

9.1. The first phase of Anglicanism – The Sixteenth-Century Reformed Church.

For Cranmer, the Anglican Formularies, for Jewel and Hooker, Scripture is Polaris, that fixed and certain unmovable guide by which Christians should orient their lives. However, tradition and reason remain useful guides. Like the auxiliary stars of the Big Dipper, when tradition and reason are lined up, they helpfully point to the Bible's own position. Therefore, the sixteenth-century Church of England gradually, but steadily, saw itself under Elizabeth as part of the wider Reformed branch of Continental Protestantism. In terms of ecclesiology, this meant that the visible church was considered to be primarily a human institution with a divine vocation to proclaim the Gospel through Word and Sacrament. As a result, mission determined order. Recovering the Gospel meant institutional separation from the Church of Rome. Spreading the Gospel effectively in England meant the retention of the historic three-fold orders. Apostolic succession was of the *bene esse*[1] of the English Church. Apostolic teaching was of the *esse*[2].

9.2. The Second Phase of Anglicanism – The Seventeenth-Century Caroline Divines.

As exemplified by Lancelot Andrewes, William Laud and Jeremy Taylor, the theologians favoured by King Charles I and King Charles II consciously rejected the reformed ethos of the Elizabethan church. Instead, beginning with their leadership of worship at Westminster Abbey and the cathedrals but gradually spreading throughout the land, the Caroline divines shaped Anglicanism as something free from both Roman and Protestant "innovations." For them the Church of England's

---

[1] 'well-being'
[2] 'essence'

doctrine was expressed, not by the homilies or the articles, but by the prayers and ancient creeds in its liturgy. Their vision was a church where bishops as well as kings were divinely instituted, where grace flowed primarily through the sacraments, where the liturgy was to be performed with as much heavenly splendour as possible, and human wills strove to co-operate with sacramental grace so as to lead holy lives. Their commitment to the "holiness of beauty" was the genesis of what many later commentators would call "Classical Anglicanism." Committed to repristinating the belief and practices of the undivided church, the Caroline divines insisted that both the interpretation of Scripture and theological reasoning had to be in accordance with the consensus of the Fathers. For them, apostolic succession and apostolic teaching were of the *esse* of the church.

With the outbreak of civil war in 1642, both Laud (1645) and Charles I (1649) were executed, episcopacy abolished and prayer book Anglicanism proscribed. When the monarchy was eventually restored in 1660, Charles II (1630-85) also restored the Anglican Church of his father, including a new *Book of Common Prayer* moderately revised along Laudian lines (1662). Consequently, nearly 3000 Puritan clergy left the state system.

9.3. *The Third Phase of Anglicanism – Latitudarianism.*

The Glorious Revolution deposed Charles II's Roman Catholic brother James II after only three years on throne in 1688. Some 400 Anglican clergy, including the Archbishop of Canterbury, left the church, since their belief in the divine institution of kings and bishops would not allow them to swear an oath to the new sovereigns. Wearied by more than two decades of strife with the Reformed clergy who had left the Church of England upon the return of the prayer book, the new government passed the Act of Toleration (1689) that permitted with certain restrictions Trinitarian Protestants who dissented from the established Anglican parochial system to gather legally their own worshipping communities.

Having already lost those clergy who were most committed to Reformed Protestantism and now the most dedicated to the principles of the undivided church as well, the Whig leadership of the Anglican Church after the Glorious Revolution increasingly found its inspiration in the prevailing intellectual principles of the Enlightenment. As a result, the triumvirate of theological authority was reprioritized by such leading thinkers as Archbishop John Tillotson (1630-94) and John Locke (1632-1704). Now the search for simplicity of doctrine and the necessity of morality was begun through reason, whose conclusions then evaluated Scripture and church tradition. Moreover, reason itself was understood anew, as an autonomous, impartial judge, unlike reason in Cranmer and the Caroline Divines which was to be aided by grace and devotion. The Bishop of Bangor spoke for the Whig leadership when he insisted that the Church of England was a decidedly human institution that needed simply to stress Enlightenment sincerity rather than Caroline apostolicity. The end result was a church whose chief purpose was to inculcate personal morality so as to maintain public order.

9.4. The Fourth Phase of Anglicanism – The Three Streams of the Nineteenth-Century Church.

During the Nineteenth Century, three vigorous parties within the Church of England emerged, each appealing to the primacy of one of the theological authorities and the century of its dominance as the basis for its claim to be the true Anglican church. The *Low Church Evangelicals* preached a return to the sixteenth-century Reformed formularies with their insistence on the supremacy of Scripture, justification by faith as wrought by personal conversion and a life of good works as its appropriate fruit. Among the most influential were: Charles Simeon of Cambridge (1759-1836) whose earnest preaching persuaded many generations of university students to enter the ordained ministry; William Wilberforce (1759-1833), who led the battle in Parliament to abolish slavery in the British Empire; and Anthony Ashley Cooper, Earl of Shaftesbury (1801-85), who fought to improve the working and living conditions of the poor.

The *High Church Oxford Movement* produced *Tracts for the Times*, a series of publications that called the Church of England to recover its spiritual heritage as an ancient catholic institution as described and defended by the Caroline divines in the Seventeenth Century. In his contributions John Henry Newman argued that the Church of England was a *via media*, following the beliefs and practices of the early church uncorrupted either by papalism or Protestantism. In fact, Newman was the first person to coin the term "Anglicanism" as a separate branch of Christendom. Although he eventually found his own arguments unconvincing and converted to Roman Catholicism, other early Tractarians such as John Keble and E.B. Pusey remained. Using their immense scholarship, they continued to promote the Oxford Movement's vision of Anglo-Catholicism, which in the Twentieth Century would succeed in reshaping the liturgy and, indeed, the very self-understanding of much of Anglicanism.

Finally, *the Broad Church movement* responded to the advent of German biblical criticism and Darwin's theory of evolution by drawing on the Eighteenth Century's commitment to the primacy of reason in theological discourse. Listen to Benjamin Jowett in his chapter "On the Interpretation of Scripture" in the landmark book *Essays and Reviews* (1860):

> Almost all intelligent persons are agreed that the earth has existed for myriads of ages; the best informed are of opinion that the history of nations extends back some thousand years before the Mosaic chronology; recent discoveries in geology may perhaps open a further vista of existence for the human species, while it is possible, and may one day be known, that mankind spread not from one but from many centres over the globe; or as others say, that the supply of links which are at present wanting in the chain of animal life may lead to new conclusions respecting the origin of man.

> [T]he time has come when it is no longer possible to ignore the results of criticism, it is of importance that Christianity should be seen to be in harmony with them . . . It is a mischief that critical observations which any intelligent man can make for himself, should be ascribed to atheism or unbelief. It would be a strange and almost incredible thing that the Gospel, which at first made war only on the vices of mankind, should now be opposed to one of the highest and rarest of human virtues—the love of truth. And that in the present day the great object of Christianity should be, not to change the lives of men, but to prevent them from changing their opinions; that would be a singular inversion of the purposes for which Christ came into the world. The Christian religion is in a false position when all the tendencies of knowledge are opposed to it. Such a position cannot be long maintained, or can only end in the withdrawal of the educated classes from the influences of religion. What remains may be comprised in a few precepts, or rather is the expansion of a single one. *Interpret the Scripture like any other book.*

Note the essentially moralist nature of Jowett's argument. The purpose of Christianity is to inculcate virtues, not specific doctrinal beliefs. When received theological convictions conflict with the advances of science, the power of religion to encourage morality is in danger of being lost. We must adjust our religious persuasions to what intelligent people can give assent in good conscience.

The influence of the Victorian commitment to morality did not end with merely shaping the broad church movement's justification for adherence to reason. The vibrant presence of three different understandings of Anglicanism at the same time presented a national church with a significant crisis of self-understanding. If neither a common doctrinal understanding nor even a common set of worship practices held the Church of England together, what could? In the end, Victorian moralism afforded a way forward. Since each different stream of Anglicanism still emphasised the necessity of repentance and ethical renewal, all could agree that what ultimately mattered was the common end of a better people, even if they could not agree as to a common theological means to do so.

9.5. Fifth Phase. The Birth of a Communion – The Lambeth Conferences.

It was in this atmosphere of increased but competing understandings of religious devotion held together by a state church's justification as the supporter of public morality that the Anglican Communion as we know it came into being. The various Anglican missionary movements had produced daughter churches throughout the world-wide British Empire. Following Article 34, these were eventually gathered together in national churches and united with one another through the bonds of affections of their bishops, brought together at Lambeth for a conference every ten years or so since 1867. Since many denominations had often joined forces for the sake of more effective missions, the larger Protestant missionary movement also produced a greater desire for Christian unity. Sensitive to this development, the Anglican bishops meeting at Lambeth in 1888 addressed how such a reunion of the various strands of Christendom could take place.

Before reading the resolution, however, it should be noted that this was considered the basis of an ecumenical project, not the definition of Anglican ecclesiology. Hence, it contains no reference to the Prayer Book or the Articles, just to the marks of a true visible church, i.e., the pure Word, as defined by *sola Scriptura* to which the ancient Creeds testify; and the Sacraments rightly administered, namely, the dominical sacraments whose efficacy was ensured by the Words of Christ spoken in association with what he used. The episcopate is added, but since it is to be locally adapted, it means that it falls under Article 34, namely, something to be rooted in the culture of a specific community as a *bene esse* of the church, not as an *esse*. Although in good Anglican and ecumenical style, of course, the phrase is ambiguous enough that an alternate interpretation remains plausible.

Here is the famous Lambeth Quadrilateral:

Resolution 11, Lambeth Conference 1888

That, in the opinion of this Conference, the following articles supply a basis on which approach may be by God's blessing made towards home reunion:

a. The Holy Scriptures of the Old and New Testaments, as "containing all things necessary to salvation," and as being the rule and ultimate standard of faith

b. The Apostles' Creed, as the baptismal symbol; and the Nicene Creed, as the sufficient statement of the Christian faith.

c. The two sacraments ordained by Christ himself - Baptism and the Supper of the Lord – ministered with unfailing use of Christ's words of institution, and of the elements ordained by him.

d. The historic episcopate, locally adapted in the methods of its administration to the varying needs of the nations and peoples called of God into the unity of his Church.

9.6. *Sixth Phase of Anglicanism – the Current Situation.*

In the Twentieth Century we witnessed the increasing secularisation of western culture, with its growing emphasis on the church's role as the encourager of public morality. As public morality became more and more associated with civil and then human rights, the eighteenth-century emphasis on the primacy of reason over Scripture and Tradition came to dominate the other two traditions as well. Now we have Affirming Catholicism and Open Evangelicalism. In the last fifty years we have also seen the advent of Anglican Charismatics who combine a commitment to Scriptural primacy with an emphasis on personal experiential renewal.

However, rather than become a separate, fourth addition to the traditional high, low and broad Anglican church parties, they have tended to express their contributions to Anglicanism primarily through seeking to renew existing Anglo-Catholic or Evangelical groups and institutions. The major exceptions to that comment are, however, the new influential centres of missional activity founded by Anglican Charismatics such as Holy Trinity Brompton and New Wine.

So here we are today. On the one hand, we have an increasing secular mainstream Anglicanism who sees its main function as supporting public morality, rather than advocating for specific theological commitments. And, of course, an increasingly secular western society derives its public morality no longer even third-hand from the Judeo-Christian tradition, but rather from an obligation to protect the individualistic expression of self. And on the other hand, we have a renewed biblical Anglicanism, in which Evangelicals, Anglo-Catholics and Charismatics are united by a common belief in the power of the Gospel to forgive our sins, reconciling us to God through the death and resurrection of Jesus Christ so as to unite us to him and to fellow Christians now and forever. The sense of unity among these groups is so strong, that many of their adherents see themselves as personally combining all three streams together.

So on the one hand, we have a morality-driven Anglicanism mainstream which has adopted a new secular morality. On the other hand, we have a renewed historic Anglicanism with different theological stories but with a common understanding of new life in Christ and a common commitment to traditional biblical morality. What has happened as a result? Now that the nineteenth-century Anglican moral consensus has collapsed at the beginning of the Twenty-First Century, we are witnessing the slow disintegration of the Anglican Communion itself.

9.7. *Assessment*

What are the options for the future of Anglican ecclesiology?

1. Can we rely on morality? That, of course, is the revisionist hope. Just like Benjamin Jowett's contribution to *Essays and Reviews* before them, the reappraisers argue that since the dispute over doctrine at the heart of the sexuality debate is undermining people's confidence in the church as a moral agent, we must put such academic discussions to the side and gather around

mission. But what mission do they offer? The Millennial Development Goals – i.e., secular morality.

2. Can we rely on structures? No, the English Gentlemen's Club that was the Lambeth Conference had neither the rules nor the will to confront flagrant rejection of its advice. As a result, the crisis over morality has destroyed the ability of any current instrument of unity to speak for all of Anglicanism. And here the Fellowship of Confessing Anglicans itself must be wary. A reliance on structure, rather than substance, is what got the Anglican Communion into the current mess. Morality apart from a common relationship with Jesus Christ cannot hold a Christian community together.

3. Can we rely on our Anglican heritage? That is the question before us. We have a motley inheritance. No group identifies with all parts of our past!

Nevertheless, let me take a personal privilege to make some suggestions on the way forward.

a. Article 19 makes clear that the church is above all else the fruit of mission. The Anglican church must be rooted in the absolute primacy of the power of the Gospel to create, sustain, renew, reform, enlarge, deepen, and eventually bring home into eternal unity the church militant with the church triumphant.

b. Article 11 makes clear that for Anglicans the Gospel is grounded in the good news of justification by faith which permits our unity with God and each other in this earthly life, despite our blemishes, both personal and corporate.

c. Article 20 makes clear that the first task of the Church is to witness to Scripture's saving message and protect Scripture's authority to define it. Article 8 reminds us that the power of the Creeds is derived from their accurate witness to and summary of the teachings of Scripture.

d. That all biblical Anglicans can agree that the true visible church, by proclaiming the Gospel through Word and Sacrament, is the ordinary means by which the mystical church is called into being, and because of that divine vocation, God is present in its midst and works through it, being faithful eventually at the end of time to unite the Eucharistic Fellowship of the institutional church with his eternal Heavenly Banquet of the mystical.

e. That despite its divine vocation, a true earthly church is still a thoroughly human institution, subject to error (Article 20) and intended by God's design to be rooted in the local community (Article 34). This commitment to the church as a human community in the process of redemption has both a strength and weakness – like human nature itself!

f. As a human community in need of redemption, the church as God's instrument of mission is called upon to use theological reason (i.e., as guided by the Holy Spirit through Scripture and tradition) to inculcate the unchanging Gospel into the specific cultures of an individual human community. That's how we ended up with both Royal Supremacy in the Sixteenth Century in the UK and the separation of Church and State in the Eighteenth Century in the USA. That's why we have such a wonderful diversity of Anglican expressions gathered together at this conference. Here is the strength of understanding the visible church as primarily a human institution.

g. However, there is a significant weakness to this approach as well. As we have seen, effectiveness in mission is the highest historic priority in Anglicanism, for the church derives its existence, purpose and power from the faithful proclamation of the gospel in word and sacrament. Because of this divine call, the church has God's assurance of his abiding presence among his people. Nevertheless, since the church as a human institution can err, the theological reasoning necessary for adapting the proclamation of the Gospel to a specific culture can all too often lead to each culture adapting and changing the Gospel to their own human idolatries. Therefore, a global fellowship is necessary to help individual national churches to discern whether a specific gospel proclamation is an effective adaptation to culture or merely a capitulation to it.

h. Finally, we need to take seriously the problem of our Erastian inheritance. The ethos of Anglicanism is as the definer and defender of a culture's morality, whether *de juro* in England or merely *de facto* in many other, but not all, provinces around the Globe. While this position in human society has in the past undoubtedly greatly aided Anglicanism's platform for gospel mission, the world has changed. Now that very instinct, too often that very need, to be the cultural leader in matters of morality, seriously undermines Anglicanism's witness to the Gospel, because western culture has by and large abandoned biblical morality. We must turn once again to Article 34 and realize that to proclaim the Gospel to current culture, we must use theological reason once again to learn how to become a post-Constantinian church.

What would that look like for Anglicanism?

- a fellowship of national churches confessing a common statement of biblical faith like the Jerusalem Declaration, rather than seeking to be the guardians of western secular morality sharing a common structure of catholic order as, at the least, the *bene esse* of the church

- exercising between the national churches the ecclesiastical discipline implied in Article 19's phrase the sacraments "duly administered" and made explicit in the rubrics of the prayer books. For as a human institution, albeit with a divine vocation, the provinces need the fellowship of each other to help and guide them to maintain a true understanding of the Gospel.

- sending forth in mission the various Anglican expressions of orthodox Christian faith to be the church in local communities.

What will be the result?

If the FCA merely clings to a common morality and a mutual rejection of neo-colonial imperialism, God will not express his mission imperative through us, and all our efforts will flounder in the end. However, if we will devote ourselves to inculcating the Gospel in our lives and life together, both as individuals and as ecclesial communities at all levels, from local to international, then whatever happens in the larger Anglican Communion will be of decidedly less importance. For then FCA's witness to the Gospel in Word and deed will stand the test of time, come what may, whether as the agent which will have renewed the wider Communion, or as the enduring expression of Anglicanism which outlasted it.

In conclusion, "mission," I say, "mission." Mission in our hearts, in our heads, in our hands, in our hopes, in our failures, in our dreams, in all our lives and at our death, mission. For mission has always been the essential DNA of authentic Anglicanism, since mission is the very nature of God's active presence in our midst as the church militant.

Thanks be to God, our Lord will not rest until we and all that are his are revealed as the church triumphant for all eternity.

10. Sea Change in the Anglican Communion: GAFCON and Communion Governance

The Revd Prof. Stephen Noll

There has been a sea change in the Anglican Communion over the past two decades. The vestments may be the same, the assorted "reverend" titles untouched, the website still showing smiling Global South Anglican faces. The reality is far different. The foundation of Anglican identity has been shaken, and with the Psalmist, many rightly wonder: "if the foundations are destroyed, what can the righteous do?" (Psalm 11:3).

The presenting cause of this sea change, as is widely known, is the acceptance and promotion of homosexuality and the redefinition of marriage. For 350 years, Anglican weddings in England and abroad have begun with these words:

> Dearly beloved, we are gathered together here in the sight of God, and in the face of this congregation, to join together this Man and this Woman in holy Matrimony; which is an honourable estate, instituted of God in the time of man's innocency, signifying unto us the mystical union that is betwixt Christ and his Church.

When this doctrine of Holy Matrimony was challenged in the 1990s by gay-rights advocates in two Anglican Provinces – The Episcopal Church USA (TEC) and the Anglican Church of Canada (ACoC) – the Lambeth Conference of bishops answered decisively that

> This Conference, in view of the teaching of Scripture, upholds faithfulness in marriage between a man and a woman in lifelong union, and believes that abstinence is right for those who are not called to marriage. (Resolution I.10)

The Lambeth Resolution led to a decade of strife within the Communion as the North Americans flatly rejected its norm and now are on the brink of providing official same-sex marriage rites. In the UK, same-sex marriage has now been signed into law by the Queen, and the Prime Minister vows to export it to the Commonwealth partners. While the Church of England has not approved same-sex marriage, the Archbishop of Canterbury argues that same-sex civil unions are a neglected moral obligation: "It is clearly essential that stable and faithful same sex relationships should, where those involved want it, be

THE TRUTH SHALL SET YOU FREE

recognised and supported with as much dignity and the same legal effect as marriage" (Speech in House of Lords, 3 June 2013).

But isn't sex outside marriage "incompatible with Scripture" (1998 Lambeth Resolution I.10; cf. Resolutions III.1 and III.5)? Indeed the larger question underlying the sexuality debate entails the authority of the Bible. To which question Presiding Bishop Katherine Jefferts Schori replies, channelling her inner Humpty Dumpty: "When I use the Word, it means just what I choose it to mean – neither more nor less." Or so it seems, as Bishop Schori interprets St. Paul's exorcism of a slave girl, oppressed by demonic and human masters (Acts 16:16-18):

> Paul can't abide something he won't see as beautiful or holy, so he tries to destroy it. It gets him thrown in prison. That's pretty much where he's put himself by his own refusal to recognize that she, too, shares in God's nature, just as much as he does – maybe more so!

Permit me, as a biblical scholar and defrocked (by TEC) priest, to protest: that an apostolic leader can twist the text of Scripture and rebuke St. Paul as she does is emblematic of the false Gospel rampant in her church, and that she remains unrebuked by and in good standing with her elders in the Communion is emblematic of the utter dysfunction of that body. In what sense can one call it a "Communion" when such denial of the faith passes for normal?

10.1. Communion Governance

This essay is not about hermeneutics or sexuality but about "ecclesiastical polity": how the Church constitutes and organizes its common life. But the two topics are linked; indeed the sea change in theology has caused a sea change in Communion governance as well.

In classical political theory, there are only so many models of polity: rule by one, rule by the few, and rule by the many. Aristotle commended a mixed polity as the most feasible of regimes, but a mixed regime is not the same as a mixed-up regime; it must have a coherent rationale, as in the instance of constitutional republics.

Classical theorists were doubtful about how far genuine polity could extend beyond a particular city or nation, into what we now call international relations. The Church, however, is by its mission charter a worldwide institution, stretching to the ends of the earth, and the

Anglican Communion, with churches "locally adapted" to their regions, reflects that global character better than many other church bodies.

I will argue that there are three basic models of Communion governance: a loose association of purely autonomous Provinces, a conciliar communion of churches, and an executive bureaucracy.

10.2. First Model: Pure Autonomy

One could argue that pure autonomy is the starting point of Anglican polity, going back to Henry VIII's detaching the national church from the Roman See. "Provincial" autonomy, usually following national boundaries, is a bedrock principle of the Anglican Communion. It was not always so. When the English began founding overseas colonies, the Church of England maintained control from afar. This policy weakened the Anglican Church in the American colonies and led to the formation of independent Methodist and Episcopal churches there. Other colonial churches remained formally tethered to the Mother Church, which eventually awarded them missionary bishops and provincial synods.

The calling of the first Lambeth Conference in 1867 was precipitated by a theological and political crisis in South Africa – the so-called Colenso affair. The meeting of 76 bishops established two precedents: that "provinces" would be organized on a one-per-region basis as recognized by the Archbishop of Canterbury; and that the "conference" of bishops would have no legal authority within England or other jurisdictions. Both these precedents continue to this day. Although there are a few anomalous overlapping jurisdictions, the 38 listed provinces are the only "official" churches of the Communion. And while there have been proposals for structuring the Communion more formally – e.g., in 1930, more of which below, these proposals have been stillborn.

Once a geographical province is recognized, are there any limits on its autonomy in terms of doctrine, discipline and worship? The answer is, theoretically, yes. The American Prayer Book (1789) states that liturgical alterations are acceptable "provided the substance of the Faith be kept entire." The first Lambeth Conference took a similar stance: while allowing for liturgical adaptation, it stated that "it is necessary that [provinces] receive and maintain without alteration the standards of the faith and doctrine as now in use in that [the Mother] Church" (Resolution 8).

The 1930 Report on the Anglican Communion poses the nightmare scenario of a church exercising its freedom and departing the faith:

> This freedom naturally and necessarily carries with it the risk of divergence to the point even of disruption. In case any such risk should actually arise, it is clear that the Lambeth Conference as such could not take any disciplinary action. Formal action would belong to the several Churches of the Anglican Communion individually; but the advice of the Lambeth Conference, sought before action is taken by the constituent Churches, would carry very great moral weight. And we believe in the Holy Spirit. We trust in His power working in every part of His Church to hold us together.

The conclusion from 1930 is that the Anglican Communion per se has no authority to deal with heresy and schism and leaves any action to each autonomous province. Nevertheless, the "moral weight" of Christian unity did indeed work as hoped – until recently.

The Episcopal Church USA and Anglican Church of Canada are the nightmare come true. Repeatedly boasting of their provincial autonomy, the North Americans obstructed the will of the larger Communion with little more than insincere expressions of "regret" and porous "moratoria" which expire whenever the next bishop or diocese decides to take "prophetic" action, e.g. in adding "transgender rights" to marriage and ordination.

Given their functional autonomy, one might ask why these churches care to remain in the Communion. The truth is, their radical agenda is transnational and they believe they can eventually infiltrate the official structures and divide and conquer the poorer churches of the Communion. If the Communion bodies were somehow to fight back and exercise discipline in such a way that these churches had to choose between conforming to its standards and "walking apart," they would separate and take some of their client churches with them.

While the crisis of the last decade has in some ways united churches of the Global South, they too are tempted to throw up their hands in frustration and operate autonomously. These churches have their own independent constitutions and have been growing without significant help from the West. They do not have funds, unless lured from the Western coffers, to travel worldwide to international meetings. The radical agenda has been, at least until recently, foreign to their culture, and they face greater challenges from Islam and Pentecostalism. "No more meetings," some say, "let's just mind the church here at home." Ironically, this attitude opens the door for TEC and ACoC to enter the Global South, bribing weaker members with "development aid."

The sea change in theology has weakened the ties that bind Anglicans around the world and raised the question whether "Communion" is not an empty label. There is nothing inherently wrong with autonomous governance of a church so long as it preserves the faith intact. Many Protestant and free church bodies operate this way. Such autonomy does, however, fall short of the ideal of a worldwide Communion expressed in Ellerton's famous hymn:

> As o'er each continent and island
> The dawn leads on another day,
> The voice of prayer is never silent,
> Nor dies the strain of praise away.

10.3. Second Model: The Conciliar Authority of Bishops

The model of ecclesiastical polity which I think best reflects the role of the historic episcopate in Anglicanism, is *rule by bishops in council*. "Conciliarity" can mean a variety of things. It does not mean the absolute authority of bishops, either independently or collegially. Bishops are responsible to the whole church through their diocesan synods of clergy and laity, and Primates are responsible to their provincial synods. Nevertheless, the historic tradition of the church has always granted bishops a special role in matters of doctrine and discipline. In terms of ecclesiology, the idea of the church being guided by bishops begins with the Council of Jerusalem in Acts 15 and proceeds to the ecumenical councils of the undivided church.

The Great Schism in 1054 and the rise of papalism in the late Middle Ages introduced an alternative form of church order among Roman Catholics, although recollections of conciliar governance surfaced briefly at the Council of Constance (1414-1418). The Reformers, including Thomas Cranmer, held out some hope for a Protestant general council, but dominance of the autonomous state church model in Europe prevented its implementation.

The advent of the Anglican Communion in the mid-19th century necessitated a rethinking of authority in Anglicanism. Several promoters of the first Lambeth Conference hoped to convene a council of bishops that would deal with specific concerns for doctrine and discipline raised by Bishop Colenso's attack on biblical authority. While Archbishop Longley certainly accepted that bishops were the proper invitees, he steered the meeting clear of being considered a council by declaring it a "conference" only, with no authority over the autonomous churches, especially the Church of England. Hence as Paul Valliere notes, "the Lambeth Conference is a living monument to Anglican ambivalence about conciliarism. The gatherings at Lambeth look like episcopal councils, yet they are not. In fact, they were purposely designed not to be councils."

There were periodic attempts by Anglicans to identify the Anglican Communion as conciliar in character, the most important of these coming to the Lambeth Conference in 1930. Lambeth 1930 is best known for its adoption of the definition of the Communion as "a fellowship, within the One Holy Catholic and Apostolic Church, of those duly constituted Dioceses, Provinces or Regional Churches in communion with the See of Canterbury" (Resolution 49). The Resolution was accompanied by a Report on The Anglican Communion, which was commended but not formally adopted by the Conference.

The Report attempts to describe the essence of Anglican Communion governance thus:

a. The Anglican Communion sees itself as part of the wider catholic, apostolic and missionary church, which has arisen out of the historical accidents of the divisions within Christendom but which is ecumenical in its hope of final reunion.

b. The Communion's identity as "Anglican" is an accident of its derivation from the British Isles, but the flourishing young churches of the Communion have now become autonomous. This statement, in my view, demystifies the idea of churches being "in communion with the See of Canterbury." It is the historical connection, the "jurisdiction of honour," that binds the churches of the Communion together with Canterbury.

c. Of the two available paradigms – Rome and Orthodoxy – the Communion is likened to the latter, which is seen to be the more ancient, as "the first four centuries were bound together by no administrative bond."

d. Conciliarity is not inconsistent with regional autonomy in matters of governance, because the churches are bound together spiritually by a common faith and practice.

So what differentiates conciliarism as a form of governance from a confederation of purely autonomous Provinces? The answer, it seems to me, is that conciliar governance involves *common consent to an agreed upon deposit of faith and worship and mutual submission of elders in the Spirit*. The common faith of the church involves a "concordant" reading of Scripture – "the rule of faith" – epitomized in the ecumenical creeds and historic confessions. The ecumenical Creeds carry the weight of the ages and the authority of the undivided church; the confessions reflect the more particular reading of that deposit within a particular historic tradition.

In the case of the Anglican Communion, the common deposit of faith is summarized in the Lambeth Quadrilateral (looking outward to other traditions) and the Thirty-Nine Articles and Book of Common Prayer (looking inward to those in our own tradition). The 1662 Prayer Book and the Articles carry the weight of having stood the test of time in an historical tradition. Occasions arise, however, where the church must address new issues either with a one-off injunction like the Lambeth Resolution I.10 of 1998 on Human Sexuality or with a new statement of faith, like the Jerusalem Declaration of GAFCON 2008. And all are to be continually tested for their conformity to the Scripture (Acts 17:11).

The proper instruments of conciliar governance in Anglicanism have been the Lambeth Conference of bishops and the Primates' "Meeting." The role of the former body is well-established. Despite the ambiguities of its start, the Lambeth Conference has functioned as a moral and spiritual authority for a century and a half. It is the very rejection of that authority following 1998 that has thrown the Communion into disarray. The Primates' Meeting had a murky beginning, but a series of Lambeth resolutions from 1978 to 1998 speak of the "enhanced role" of the Primates in Communion governance. According to the Virginia Report (§6.32 [1995]) and the Windsor Report (§65 [2005]), the Primates have an *inherent authority* grounded in the role of bishops as successors of the apostles. This authority is not merely a matter of institutional power, but of the truth of the apostolic gospel transmitted through the Scripture and the offices of the Church.

In my opinion, the conciliar model has the strongest claim among others as the foundation for Anglican Communion governance in a post-colonial era and has roots in the development of the Anglican Communion. However a different model has grown up in the past few years that undermines true conciliarity.

10.4. *Third Model: The Lambeth Bureaucracy*

The third model, the executive bureaucracy, is the most common secular regime today, from totalitarian versions in the former Soviet Union and China to soft-power versions in Europe and North America. In an executive bureaucracy, it is often difficult to discern who exercises the greater power, the chief executive or the bureaucrats. In fact, when running well, the executive and the bureaucracy operate hand in glove.

In the case of the Anglican Communion, I use the phrase "Lambeth bureaucracy" because it combines two elements: the historical (and colonial) role of the Archbishop of Canterbury as first bishop among equals, with the American project of building a centralized bureaucracy. The key component of the bureaucracy is the Anglican Communion Office (ACO) and its chief administrator, the Secretary General. The wheels of the bureaucracy are greased with money, coming primarily from the United States and the UK.

Like any of its secular counterparts, the Lambeth bureaucracy pretends to be a broadly representative servant ministry. It is not. One striking feature of the ACO is the overwhelmingly lily-white complexion of its staff, which is probably less a matter of overt racism than a reflection of the old-boy network that requires purebred bureaucrats to come from the Anglo-American stable. Many contemporary bureaucracies employ methods of manipulation to maintain power and achieve their ends. In the case of the Lambeth bureaucracy, the official method is called "*indaba*." Despite its African etymology with an aura of communal wisdom, *indaba* is in practice a means to *manipulate* opinion and results. The preparation of agenda, the writing of reports, the control of media all require careful oversight by "professionals," who happen also to be committed to the bureaucratic status quo.

One may wonder whether the primacy of the Archbishop of Canterbury might be a check against the Communion Office. Theoretically yes perhaps, but actually not. Even the Bishop of Rome, whose primacy is theologically grounded, has difficulty overcoming the Vatican bureaucracy. The Archbishop of Canterbury is as enmeshed in the Lambeth bureaucracy as he is in the British Establishment, which explains why the recent change of Archbishops has resulted in no change in policies at the top.

Can executive bureaucracy be an authentic form of Communion governance? Certainly: the Pope and Vatican have functioned successfully for half a millennium. But the Vatican, unlike Lambeth, makes no pretence that its worldwide churches are autonomous or that there is no central authority in its ecclesiastical governance. Equally important, the Roman bureaucracy has resisted letting the forces of revisionism spin out of control. The current Lambeth bureaucracy, by contrast, has been protecting its liberal constituencies over the past decade and has done so at a high cost: alienation of a huge bloc of churches. Finally, for all the mystery of insider politics, Rome has found a way to elect pontiffs who are non-Italian and represent genuinely global concerns, whereas the Lambeth bureaucracy is still legally, politically, and ideologically tied to England and the secular West. It is significant that in 2012, the Primate chosen to represent the wider Anglican Communion on the Crown Nominations Commission, the body that nominated the current Archbishop of Canterbury, was Dr Barry Morgan, Primate of The Church in Wales, whose theological views are greatly at odds with the Global South churches.

10.5. The Ebb and Flow of Communion Power 1998-2008

Lambeth Resolution I.10 represented not only a theological watershed in Anglican history but a political one as well. The Lambeth Conference of bishops by a wide majority had expressed itself on a central matter of Christian faith and morality. The two churches most directly affected exercised their autonomy to reject that authority. Indeed, in 2003, the Episcopal Church authorized and its Primate presided at the consecration of a practicing homosexual bishop, V. Gene Robinson. For the first time in its history – at least since its formation in 1867 – the Communion faced a critical question: could it discipline a member church that openly violated Communion and biblical norms?

The burden of this question fell on the Primates, who met in 2000, 2002, 2003, 2005 and 2007 to respond to the reaction, inaction and provocative action of The Episcopal Church. The Lambeth bureaucracy ran interference for TEC, turning aside a concrete proposal for discipline ("To Mend the Net") and setting up a "Windsor Process" that delayed action by the Primates for four years. Meeting in Dar es Salaam in 2007, the Primates, led by Abp. Peter Akinola, finally issued a communiqué with concrete conditions and an ultimate sanction of exclusion from Communion bodies. Although he was a signatory to the communiqué, the Archbishop of Canterbury reneged on applying the key sanctions. In particular, he proceeded to invite all the TEC bishops (except Gene Robinson) to attend Lambeth 2008 as full members – and this in spite of warnings from Global South churches that they would boycott the meeting if he did so.

The die was cast. The Lambeth bureaucracy proceeded to smother the Lambeth Conference – minus 280 bishops – with meaningless *indaba* interspersed by primatial addresses from Canterbury. The Archbishop made it clear that the Primates had overstepped their authority and would subsequently be confined to the plantation of friendly conversation. On the other side, the Primates and bishops of seven Provinces attended the Global Anglican Future Conference (GAFCON) in Jerusalem in 2008 and have attended Communion functions sporadically in the years since.

The tide of conciliar governance had flowed to the full at Lambeth 1998. By 2008, one could hear its long, withdrawing roar from the shores of Albion, soon to break anew on the coasts of the Levant and Africa.

10.6. GAFCON and the Future of the Anglican Communion

It is my contention that in the past fifteen years, a sea change has come to the Anglican Communion, which has moved from conflict to crisis to dissolution. The Anglican Communion of Ellerton's hymn is no more. Yeats' vision is closer to reality: "things fall apart, the centre cannot hold." The tide of postmodern scepticism has undermined the sea-wall of Anglican collegiality and deference to tradition and has flooded some of the most prestigious churches, even as a new tide of the Spirit has been rising in the Global South. The "Instruments of Unity" have failed to guard the faith and unity of the Church and in many cases have collaborated in promoting a false gospel. It is not possible to go back. Hence the importance of the GAFCON movement.

GAFCON 2008 was remarkable in many ways. Organized at short notice and on a modest budget, it drew more than 1,000 bishops, clergy and laypeople from 35 countries to the historic birthplace of the church, Jerusalem. The Conference included inter-cultural fellowship, various topical seminars, lively worship, and pilgrimages to the holy places of Jesus and the apostles.

GAFCON 2008 was not merely a conference. Whereas the 2008 Lambeth Conference carefully avoided any decision making, GAFCON acted 'synodally', to borrow a term from Bishop Michael Nazir Ali, and produced a succinct Statement, which did the following:

- It judged that the Anglican Communion was threatened by a departure from the truth of the Gospel and that the existing "Instruments" had proved unable or unwilling to deal this crisis.

- It claimed not to depart from the Anglican Communion but "to reform, heal and revitalise the Anglican Communion and expand its mission to the world."

- It grounded its authority on the primary authority of Scripture, the creeds and councils of the ancient church, the Reformation Articles of Religion, and a contemporary statement of faith, the Jerusalem Declaration.

- It formed a GAFCON Primates' Council and invited the Anglican Church in North America (ACNA) to seek official recognition and membership on the Council.

- It formed a network, known as the Global Fellowship of Confessing Anglicans.

The GAFCON Statement and Jerusalem Declaration were developed under the supervision of the seven Primates present and in collaboration with bishops, scholars and other church leaders present. It was joyfully affirmed in a plenary session of 1200 participants on the last day of the Conference.

The Global Fellowship of Confessing Anglicans (GFCA) is still a fledgling body, and the Lambeth establishment has studiously ignored its existence. Nevertheless, its Primates Council has met semi-annually for the past five years. In 2010, the Council recognized the Anglican Church in North America as a legitimate member of the Communion and welcomed its Archbishop, Robert Duncan, as a full member of the Council. Some additional Global South leaders have attended GFCA functions as observers, and many have legitimated the orders of clergy from ACNA who had been defrocked (the present writer included) and thrown out of their churches. GFCA has also authorized the ordination of four deacons (in Kenya) to serve the "Anglican Mission in England."

The burden of my argument is that the GFCA holds the key – and the only key – to a genuinely conciliar form of Communion governance and the only possible alternative to the Lambeth bureaucracy. The upcoming GAFCON 2013 meeting in Nairobi will be the occasion whereby the movement goes forward, or possibly stalls.

In my view, the next crucial step to take is for GFCA churches to differentiate themselves from the Lambeth "Instruments" and re-form an Anglican polity along these lines:

1. GFCA understands itself not as departing from the Anglican Communion but rather reconstituting Anglican polity on a theological, missional, and post-colonial basis. God has given and empowered a vision of the global Anglican future in the rise of evangelical, Spirit-led Christianity among Anglicans in the Global South over the past half-century. The GAFCON movement is a response to that vision and is a truly global fellowship.

2. GFCA proclaims that true Anglican identity is based on the "faith once for all delivered to the saints." This faith is grounded in the Scriptures, preserved in the Church's creeds, formularies and liturgies, and adapted locally in the various contexts of mission. GFCA has offered the Jerusalem Statement and Declaration as a statement of the faith relevant to the future development of the Anglican Communion and normative for its members.

3. GFCA churches and bishops will build internal solidarity and loyalty to the GAFCON movement and the Jerusalem Declaration. One practical step will be for a majority of bishops and other key representatives from each member Province to meet at GAFCON 2013. In particular, a bishops' assembly should begin to see itself as a deliberative body.

4. GFCA member churches will look to its Primates Council as the ecclesiastical authority in matters of doctrine, discipline, and worship, even if some Primates continue to attend the Lambeth Primates' Meeting.

5. GFCA will establish networks and most likely a representative body of members of different ranks and ages to meet its collective mission. Much of the collaborative work will be accomplished through networks addressing specific needs, such as education (at all levels), evangelism, development, and public policy.

6. GFCA Primates Council will identify a presiding primate, as it has been doing, on the basis of seniority and giftedness rather than being rooted in a particular see. It will commit adequate

funds and manpower to an effective secretariat to carry forward the work of the Fellowship.

7. GFCA will continue to accord the Archbishop of Canterbury a "primacy of honour" and work with him, where possible, for the renewal of the Christian faith in England and its daughter churches. GFCA will seek to build authentic ecumenical relations inside and outside the Anglican fold, including the existing Anglican "Instruments" and non-GFCA provinces. While the Archbishop has not to date publicly recognized the fact that a second polity has emerged under the aegis of the Communion, it would be a bold and welcome step out of the institutional boat if he did.

This agenda expresses my own personal aspiration for the polity of the Global Fellowship of Confessing Anglicans. Rome was not built in a day, and no doubt a reformed and renewed Communion will emerge over time, under the mercy of God, from the prayers and wisdom of many others. The upcoming GAFCON 2013 Conference will set many different matters before its membership. It is my conviction that reconstituting the Communion, which was begun dramatically at the first Conference in 2008, will be a piece of its on-going work, fulfilling its high calling to be "not just a moment in time, but a movement in the Spirit."

11. GAFCON and the East African Revival Context

Dr Colin Reed

The GAFCON Jerusalem Statement of 2008 expressed sorrow over the 'acceptance and promotion within the Provinces of the Anglican Communion of a different gospel ... which is contrary to the apostolic gospel'. It noted with regret the 'failure of the Communion instruments to exercise discipline in the face of overt heterodoxy'. The Jerusalem Declaration made clear the aim of GAFCON 'to chart a way forward together that protects and promotes the biblical gospel and mission to the world'. It then clarified the key beliefs for which the movement stands. We may summarise these as:

- The gospel of salvation by God's grace through faith in Jesus Christ

- The Scriptures as the 'Word of God written' which contains 'all things necessary for salvation'

- The historic Creeds and the 39 Articles and the 1662 *Book of Common Prayer* (BCP) 'as a true and authoritative standard of worship and prayer'.

- The unique and universal Lordship of Christ, the only Saviour who by the 'death we deserve' saves 'from sin, judgement and hell'

At the heart of GAFCON is the debate over the authority of the Scriptures and the gospel they proclaim. This is not new! It was a burning issue in the 1920s, and the Revival that swept through East Africa from the 1930s arose in part out of that debate. From the 1890s onwards there had been heated debate over the inspiration of the Bible, its historicity and reliability. Was it in fact the authoritative Word of God? A new wave of a more 'liberal' view of the Scriptures spread in theological institutions in the Western world and therefore in the church, expressing the view that the Bible consisted of documents which were helpful but not necessarily actually true or definitive for faith. As it did so, so did a vigorous movement determined to uphold the authority and reliability of the Bible. Inevitably, this led to division as the lines were drawn.

The Revival movement spread from the little country of Rwanda to Uganda, to the areas of Tanzania bordering Rwanda, to Kenya, to the eastern part of the Congo. It would help to shape the theology and worship of the church in East Africa for many years to come. It was also to make an impact in 'the West', in Britain, America, Australia and New Zealand, through the reports of missionaries, through African visitors to those countries and through teams sent from Africa specifically to spread the dynamic of the Revival. Some church leaders from other countries also visited East Africa specifically to see the Revival for themselves.

This Revival had two aspects. First, it was in the mainstream of universal evangelical faith, and thus resonated with Christians in other places. It was Biblically based, it was centred on Christ Jesus, it had a high view of the work of Christ on the Cross. But it was also very much an African indigenous movement; 'the involvement, the rhythm, the jubilation; everything about it was genuinely African'.[1] It also addressed issues in African culture from inside, and thus with an authority which missionaries did not have. It was thus in keeping with the 34th Article of the BCP 'Of the Traditions of the Church' which laid down the principle that in the Anglican Church it was not necessary for the church in every place to have identical 'Traditions and Ceremonies' and each national church has the authority to adopt suitable ceremonies as long as 'nothing be ordained against God's Word'.

To understand the Revival we need to have some insight into both aspects; the wider Christian faith with which the Revival was connected, and its specific African nature. We need to look at the background from which the missionaries came, those who had founded the Anglican Church in East Africa. Their contribution to African Christianity is therefore important. But one of the strengths of the Revival was that it was led predominantly by Africans and expressed itself in African cultural forms. This was an era when many 'independent African churches' were coming into being, in the desire to understand the faith in an African manner, and express it in appropriate cultural forms independent of foreign control. The Revival had many features in common with these churches, but was determined not to secede from the denominational church. This too is an important feature of this Revival movement. In this too, it is a helpful model for today. It was a movement of revival within the church and of evangelism from the church.

---

[1]   B Sundkler, Bara Bukoba, *Church and Community in Tanzania* (London, C Hurst & Co, 1980) p 115

In the controversy over the Bible and the Gospel in the 1920s one of the first arenas in which evangelicals saw the differences as irreconcilable and so went their different ways was in the student Christian movement in the United States, in Britain and later in Australia. Shortly before the start of the First World War the avowedly Evangelical and Biblical sections of the student movement separated from the more 'liberal' Student Christian Movement. Leading the new Christian Union movement was the Cambridge Inter-Collegiate Christian Union (CICCU). This was the training ground of many of the missionaries in East Africa and their supporters, and especially those of the Rwanda Mission (and of Archbishop Howard Mowll of Sydney, who visited East Africa).

There was also to be division in the major Anglican mission organisation, the Church Missionary Society, an Evangelical Society. Now the new theology began to affect the CMS as some of its leaders expressed doubts about the historicity of the Bible. In 1921 a group of missionaries and mission supporters split off from CMS to found the Bible Churchmen's Missionary Society, committed to the belief that the Bible is the inerrant and inspired Word of God. BCMS also considered setting up a branch in Australia but did not do so, as the CMS there remained committed to Biblical truth.

Those who founded the CMS Rwanda Mission in the same year shared the same concern. This Mission became a self-governing body within the Society, and expected its missionaries to be fully committed to Biblical truth and authority. During World War I a couple of young English doctors had served with the British Army in East Africa and had a deep concern for the colonies which had been German but were given to Belgium after the war, Rwanda and Burundi. These two doctors, Algie Stanley Smith and his wife Zoe, and Len Sharpe and his wife Esther, became the first missionaries of the new Mission. They were initially located in the south-west of Uganda as the Belgian authorities would not give them permission to live in Rwanda. Both were graduates of Cambridge University and had been members of the Christian Union.

Another major influence in the evangelical world was the 'Keswick' movement which had offshoots in Australia. In 1875 a group started the first of the conventions at Keswick in the north of England which gave the movement its name. They were committed to teaching and living out a life of total commitment to God through Christ. Holiness of life was the aim, the victory over sin and temptation. Full surrender was a catch-cry. The missionary movement was deeply influenced by this and most of the missionaries had accepted its intense spirituality.

Although the Gospel had been brought by missionaries, Africans were not passive; they either accepted the new message or were opposed to it. The story of Uganda's early martyrs had spread widely not only in Uganda but in the Western world. The first few CMS missionaries had gone to Uganda in the late 1870s and they were soon followed by Roman Catholic missionaries, the 'White Fathers'. The young king of Buganda[2] was not sure how to react to the coming of these representatives of the outside world and was suspicious of their motives. He ordered the execution of the first Anglican bishop of East Africa, James Hannington, in 1885 and then turned on those who had accepted the new faith. Many were killed over the next months. Most of these were youngsters from the king's extensive court, sons and daughters of chiefs. They had become 'readers'; they had learnt to read and the texts they used were passages of Scripture. So to be a Christian (in the Anglican tradition) was in Uganda to be a reader of Scripture. It was also to accept the possibility of martyrdom. From Buganda the Gospel message had spread, largely through the witness of ordinary Christians who wanted to share their new faith.

In the 1930s the centre of the early stage of the Revival was Gahini, a small new mission station in Rwanda. In 1928 Joe Church had come to work there, alongside the earlier missionaries. He was to become a leading missionary figure in the Revival, alongside the African leaders. He too was also a product of Cambridge, the CICCU and of Keswick.

Just after Christmas, 1933, the missionaries had organised a conference at Gahini.[3] The Bible teaching was orthodox, well presented, and led to little apparent response. Both missionaries and African Christians had hoped for something more vital. So it was agreed to extend the event for a further day, especially for prayer. This started with somewhat formal prayers, then unexpectedly one of the African Christians stood and completely changed the mood. He spoke earnestly of what he saw as a personal conviction of his sinfulness, of God

---

[2] Buganda is the homeland of the Baganda people whose language is Luganda. It is part of modern Uganda, which at that time was made up of four major kingdoms and other areas in which there were no kings but councils of elders.

[3] P. St John, *Breath of Life: The Story of the Ruanda Mission* (London, The Norfolk Press, 1971) p 108.

requiring changes in his life. He began to confess openly what he saw as his sins. With tears, he publicly revealed the things that burdened his conscience. The atmosphere became electric; person after person stood and followed suit. They confessed their perceived sins, sometimes two or three speaking at a time, as a wave of spiritual conviction swept through the group.[4]

This may perhaps be seen as the beginning of the movement. It was to set the scene for what was to follow as the Revival spread. Repentance was a key theme; repentance as people came under a deep conviction of their sinfulness and had a vision of the Saviour who died for them. Sometimes this vision was vivid and dramatic, as in the case of one who was to become a leader in the movement, Festo Kivengere. 'Suddenly, as if in a vision, in front of me was Jesus hanging on the cross, as clear as anything I have seen with my physical eyes'.[5] The acceptance of God's forgiveness in Christ led to much jubilation in the person themselves and in those around them. This was expressed in hugging (people of the same gender), in singing, in waving hands and in other ways. The enthusiasm was infectious. Many within the church confessed to the fact that they had conformed outwardly to the Christian Faith but had in fact continued to live lives unchanged, often admitting to sexual immorality and to continuing involvement with 'witchcraft' and practices associated with the African belief in the spirit world, such as libations to the ancestors.

The Revival was also a challenge to a more solidly Biblical faith. These two aspects can be seen in two events in the early history of the movement in Uganda. In 1936 one of the young leaders, Blasio Kigozi, made a call to the Synod of the Anglican Church in Uganda to 'Awake'.[6] He proposed three questions to put to the Synod challenging members about the spiritual state of the Church and calling for revival. He asked, what was the cause of coldness and hardness in the church, he asked why church members living immoral lives were permitted to receive Communion, and he asked what could be done about these things. This gives us an insight into the Revival view of the Church as formally correct yet making little impact on the personal lives of members.

---

[4] H.H. Osborn, *Fire in the Hills* (London, Mid Africa Ministries (CMS), 1991) p 71
[5] Osborn, *Fire in the Hills*, p 100.
[6] J. Church later wrote a brief account of Kigozi's conversion experience and call to the Church in Uganda, titled *Awake, An African Calling: The Story of Blasio Kigozi and His Vision of Revival* (London, CMS, 1936).

Perhaps some of our synods could benefit from similar questions being asked! Sadly, Kigozi died of a sudden fever on his way to the Synod. However, the questions were put and debated among some controversy.

Secondly, the concern for Biblical truth. As the Revival spread up to the capital, Kampala, so did the opposition to it. This came to a head in 1940-41 in conflict at Bishop Tucker Theological College, when Bishop Stuart invited Joe Church to lead a college mission there.[7] CMS had sent some of the missionaries who were more liberal in theology to the northern parts of Uganda, including to the staff of this college. The students who joined the *Balokole*[8] were vocal in their criticisms of what they saw as a lack of spiritual life among their fellow students and among the staff. A missionary lecturer in Theology felt that some of their complaints of theological liberalism were aimed at him personally. He retaliated by banning meetings of the 'Brethren'. They refused to comply.[9] He then dismissed twenty-six students, and the college chaplain who had allied himself with them.[10] Among those dismissed was William Nagenda, brother in law to two leaders of the Revival, Blasio Kigozi (who had recently died) and Simeoni Nsibambi. William Nagenda, now dismissed from college, was free to dedicate himself to the Revival. He was a graduate of Makerere College (the only tertiary level institution in East Africa).[11] He became one of the recognised leaders in the Revival. Unfortunately the Bishop, Stuart, who was quite sympathetic to the Revival, was out of the country at the time.

Opposition to the Revival came from some Ugandan clergy and some missionaries; the enthusiastic 'Brethren' saw the clergy as holding on to power, and as lacking spiritual life. However, the Revival gradually gained ground, and eventually became the norm of church life, so that clergy and church leaders were expected to be associated with it.

---

[7]   Nthamburi, *From Mission to Church*, p. 117, in the article by Ward, 'The Balokole Revival in Uganda'.

[8]   The Revival members were often called *Balokole* – the Saved One, (in Luganda), initially used derisively.

[9]   Shaw, M., *The Kingdom of God in Africa: A Short History of African Christianity* (Grand Rapids, Baker Books, 1996) p 252. The members of the Revival were initially called *Abaka*, 'those on fire', but from quite early on the title *Balokole*, 'saved ones', was to become more widespread.

[10]   Church, *Quest for the Highest* (ExeterUK: Paternoster Press, 1981) p 184.

[11]   Osborn, *Fire in the Hills*, p. 81. Nagenda had studied at Makerere before that institution conferred degrees, so obtained a Diploma.

Back in Rwanda, the missionary Joe Church started regular Bible teaching classes, and developed a simple book which covered key areas of doctrine, *Every Man a Bible Student*[12] This was reprinted many times and was widely used, in English and in other languages. The aim was to ensure that Christians had a sound Biblical basis. The book was basically a compilation of Bible verses relating to key areas of doctrine. (The Swahili version is still sometimes seen – *Kila Mtu Mwafunzi wa Biblia*). Again we see the emphasis on sound teaching.

From Rwanda to Uganda, to the areas of Tanganyika bordering these countries, then into Kenya the Revival spread. It arrived in Kenya in 1936 when a team from Rwanda held a convention at Kabete, near Nairobi. From there the dynamic new movement spread quickly through the areas to the north and east of the capital, Nairobi, the traditional lands of the Kikuyu and related peoples. The staff of the theological college, St Paul's, Limuru, accepted the teaching and practices of the movement and so it became customary for newly trained clergy to be part of the Revival. The Revival also spread through Western Kenya from Uganda.

11.1. *Some Marks of the Movement and its African as well as universal character*

A clear experience of salvation: repentance and restitution

The means to that salvation, as the participants perceived it, are well expressed in the central hymn of the Revival, 'the saving blood has cleansed me, glory, glory to the Lamb'.[13] The hymn reflects the Revival emphasis on personal salvation through Jesus Christ and his blood shed. The message was simple, maybe simplistic– and therein lay both its strength: it was accessible to all, and its weakness: it was theologically limited. The key text of the Revival was 1 John 1:5-2:2. Central was the verse *'if we walk in the light as he himself is in the light, we have fellowship with one another, and the blood of Jesus his Son cleanses us from all sin'*. Repentance was the first mark of the teaching and the experience; there was emphasis on the sinfulness of human nature, even of redeemed humanity. Yet it was not just that repentance was taught, rather that people were moved by personal conviction to acts of

---

[12]   J E Church, *Every Man a Bible Student* (STL 1981)
[13]   Translated from *Sankey's Sacred Songs and Solos* No.629, 'Precious Saviour'.

repentance and restitution. People experienced a sense of guilt and a desire for forgiveness and restoration. For example, in 1938 Canon Pittway (an Englishman) wrote from Nairobi of many prisoners in the jail 'publicly confessing their sins and seeking the way of Life in Christ'. He described an event typical of the Revival, a prisoner confessing to a theft, and being willing to go to the authorities to return the money which he had kept, to sell the house he had bought with the rest and return it also. In Tanzania a British District Officer wrote of having to send a lorry to a village to collect all the tools people had stolen from the government and now wished to return.

Then there was clear teaching on the efficacy of Christ's death as the sole means of being cleansed from sin, both for one wishing to become a Christian and for a person already in the faith. The leaders felt that there had been insufficient emphasis on the theology of a 'new birth' as a radical spiritual experience, of discontinuity with the past life.[14] For believers, they stressed the necessity of daily repentance and spiritual 'cleansing'. This, they believed, led to a deep sense of freedom and of joy. The Revival stressed the fact that, every day, believers could and should experience the forgiveness flowing from the Cross of Christ, and the assistance of the Holy Spirit to overcome temptation for that day.[15] Victory was to be a daily experience, not a future hope. So salvation was the key teaching of the Revival, specifically, salvation from personal sin through the 'blood of Jesus', his saving death. Repentance was both the means of entry to this experience and an on-going necessity of daily life. By these means the Christian could live in victory over evil and sin.

A strong sense of community

African perceptions of humanity are communal; individuals exist meaningfully only in so far as they have a web of relationships and roles which define them. The Revival created a very communal form of expressing the Christian Faith. At the heart of its life were 'fellowship' meetings for Bible teaching, sharing, testimonies, singing and prayer. Those in 'fellowship' visited each other in their homes to pray.

---

[14] Anderson, *The Church in East Africa 1840-1974*,(Central Tanganyika Press, 1977) p 124, quoting a letter from Blasio Kigozi to Canon Barham; 'It seems to me that my own teachers in the past never emphasised strongly enough "being born again" as a necessity for salvation'.

[15] Shaw, *The Kingdom of God in Africa*, p 252.

Members cared for one another in practical ways; a member needing specific assistance could ask the group and they would give their labour and their money to meet an agreed need. The communal aspect was almost analogous to membership of a clan or tribe. But whereas in a tribal culture only the male elders had a say in decisions, in the Revival women and youth were given a voice.

Confession and 'brokenness'

A particular feature of the movement was the emphasis on public confession of sin, in the context of a Revival gathering. This can be seen as connected to the communal nature of the movement. Repentance without public confession was seen to be inadequate and incomplete. This led to the sense of the need to live a life open before other members of the groups, including the openness to rebuke a fellow Christian or to be rebuked. Integral to this was the concept of being 'broken', putting aside pride and self and having a 'broken and a contrite spirit'. People were expected to have a personal testimony of the changes that Jesus had made in their life. As they shared this, meetings would frequently break into the Revival hymn.

Vivid preaching

There was an emphasis on the Word of God, in preaching that was colourful and vigorous, and often, in the African style, allegorical. Images, pictorial language and anecdote were widely used rather than Biblical exegetical preaching. It would be a valid criticism of the movement that the preaching was not deeply theological, but rather experiential, using the Scriptures as illustrative. Yet it should be stressed that many of the 'Brethren' were steeped in the Scriptures; the Bible shaped their thought processes and life values.

Power in the spiritual realm

The deep hold of traditional spiritual practices and the attendant fear of offending the spirits were openly spoken of and believers were exhorted to turn from all previous religious practices. The power of the Christian life to bring freedom from the fear of 'witchcraft' and its ability to cause harm through spirit manipulation was a major theme of the teaching. Thus the faith was indigenised; it faced issues in African cultures from within, in a way missionaries could not. Traditional religion was largely about power; the revival offered a greater power in Christ.

Lay leadership

The Revival fellowship was a lay-led body, and therein lay one of its strengths: it was a movement of the members. Clergy had no special function in the 'Brethren' although they were often members. Lay leadership was linked to the independence and autonomy of the movement, and was also sometimes a threat to the clergy!

Singing

Singing played an important part in the Revival. In the early days, sometimes people sang through the night. A theologian later analysing some of the popular songs and hymns commented, 'It is here that we see find the source of the *Abalakole* revival life and faith'.[16]

11.2. A message for today

There are several aspects of the East African Revival which speak to our present situation.

The Revival was a true movement of the Holy Spirit, not a human construct. It was vital, it was spontaneous. Yet it also became organised with a system of committees at various levels, local, national, even international.

The leaders sought to transform the church from within, under the power of God. So as we seek the renewal of our Communion we need to be utterly dependent on God, yet we value an organisation which enables us to act together, nationally and internationally.

The Revival remained independent, yet within the mainstream churches. It was a community, 'voluntary, spontaneous, and outside the formal structures of the Protestant Churches to which the Revivalists

---

[16] Werner Both, 'Hymns of the Abalokole Revival in Buhaya Tanzania: a preliminary theological analysis', paper presented to the Workshop in Religious Research, June 1966-June 1968, Nairobi Kenya, and reproduced in duplicated form under the title, *Theory and Practice in Church Life and Growth: 36 Studies in Eastern, Central and Southern Africa over the Past 100 Years*, pp.305-7. The name *Abalokole* (Luganda – 'The Saved Ones') was to become the most familiar name given to the 'Revival Brethren'.

belonged"[17]. Yet members remained loyal to their denominations. So the Jerusalem Declaration reminds us that as members of GAFCON 'we rejoice in our Anglican sacramental and liturgical heritage'.

The members of the movement loved the Bible and the leaders were committed to Biblical preaching and teaching. This led to real repentance, transforming lives in a dramatic manner. This was the key witness to those outside. The same passion for God's Word and its proclamation drives us.

This Revival was a powerful factor in making the faith 'at home' in Africa – no longer a foreign import, but an African faith. Yet it was true to the essentials of a Biblical Evangelicalism – Word centred, Christ centred, Cross centred. So the faith needs to be in every place, a local expression of the church universal.

Revival of the church is not our ultimate purpose, but a renewed church is a vital agent of the gospel in a dark world. So 'We gladly accept the Great Commission of our risen Lord to make disciples of all nations (Jerusalem Declaration para 9) and (para 14) 'we rejoice at the prospect of Jesus coming again in glory'.

[17] J.N.K. Mugambi, (Ed.), *A Church Come of Age: Fifty Years of Revival in the CPK Diocese of Embu, 1942-1992* (Nairobi, Acton Publishers, 1992), article by N. Kivuti, 'Fellowship and the Church Today', p. 41.

12. Standing Firm: Archbishop Eliud Wabukala's Address to the Fellowship of Confessing Anglicans, UK & Ireland

The Most Revd Eliud Wabukala

Praise the Lord! I am so pleased that you as members of the Fellowship of Confessing Anglicans in the United Kingdom and Ireland have been able to join us this evening. As leaders from some thirty different countries we have been meeting this week to discern God's will at this time of continuing crisis in the Anglican Communion. Gathering here in London, we have been much aware that, whatever our present difficulties, many of us trace back our gospel inheritance to the British Isles and you have a special and honoured place in our affections.

This evening I want to encourage you to stand firm in the faith we have received as those who have been brought together by the gospel, and are passionate to see our Anglican Communion drawing fruitfully on its Reformation inheritance, to bear witness to Jesus Christ as the unique Saviour and only Lord around the globe. There are institutional implications to the stand we are taking, but, at its heart, this is a spiritual crisis.

Here, as in much of the West and now in Africa too, you are coming under growing pressure to compromise the gospel. I recognise that you are living in a culture where it is increasingly difficult to sustain a consistent Christian witness. Sometimes laws are interpreted to inhibit Christian witness and popular opinion is often hostile to the Christian values and beliefs which have provided the historic foundation of your society. A Jesus who is just a guide and teacher along with others is deemed acceptable, but not a Jesus who is Lord – but a Jesus who is not Lord is not the Jesus of the Bible, the one who is Alpha and Omega, the crucified and risen Lord of all creation to whom be praise and glory forever!

In such times the Church should be, in the words of the Apostle Paul, a 'pillar and bulwark of the truth', (1 Timothy 3:15) but as we have heard this week, the Church of England and the other Anglican Churches of the British Isles are in spiritual crisis themselves. We have been saddened to hear this week of the all too familiar pattern of orthodox and evangelical laity, ordinands and clergy being marginalised and their witness chilled by church hierarchies that bend to the prevailing culture.

So this evening, my dear brothers and sisters, on behalf of our global fellowship, I want to encourage you to stand firm. This may or may not mean a change in church structures, depending on your circumstances, but this quality of resilient courage is vital in the spiritual crisis we face. I want to remind you of the words of the Apostle Paul as he draws to the conclusion of his first letter to the Corinthians in chapter 16, verses 13 & 14. He gives a series of short, sharp encouragements:

> Be on your guard; stand firm in the faith; be men of courage; be strong. Do everything in love.

'Be on your guard'; we must be alert lest our comfort and security becomes more important than pleasing the Lord. Unless we pay careful attention to the Scriptures and make them central to our life together, we shall lose our sensitivity to what pleases the Lord. We are given a sense of taste so that we will swallow the good and spit out the bad. Unless our taste is trained by the Word of God, we are in danger of swallowing the bad and spitting out the good. This discernment, that springs from a wholehearted love of the Lord and his Word, is so important. Remember that the Risen Christ challenges the complacency of the Laodiceans by warning them that because they are neither hot nor cold, he will 'spit them out of his mouth' (Revelation 3:16).

We need to be on guard so that we can 'stand firm in the faith'. This is not a faith we have designed or chosen to fit with our life style preferences. It is *the* faith, the faith revealed by the God who has spoken to us through his Son and graciously given us the inspired Scriptures. Standing firm requires effort. It can be costly because it calls for resistance and once we surrender to the current of popular opinion it becomes increasingly difficult to resist.

I want to urge you to see that there is no middle ground. If you do not face any immediate threats in your particular circumstances, it is tempting to think that you can opt out and keep these difficult things at arm's length, but I want to remind you that we are a Fellowship of Confessing Anglicans and we need each other. We should not exist in isolation, but even if we try to do so, the fact remains that we all witness in a context – and in your context in the British Isles, the gap between the worldview of the Scriptures and the worldview of modern secular humanism is becoming more and more clear. One or other of those narratives will frame your thinking and your action.

It is easy to state the problem, but how do we act as 'men (and women of course) of courage'? We know what physical courage looks like, and sometimes that is indeed called for, but what does this courage look like in the spiritual battle we are called to fight?

It will show itself in persistence. When things are breaking down, it is usually just a minority who are willing to recognise the problem and they will face opposition. When we were preparing for GAFCON at Jerusalem in 2008, the movement was belittled and opposed, even by some who shared our core doctrinal commitments, but we persevered and by God's grace we were privileged to be part of an historic moment in the reshaping of our Communion for the twenty-first century.

The story of the ACNA has been one of persevering faith from small beginnings despite relentless litigation in North America. Here in the British Isles there is a reluctance to go to law against those who are seen as dissidents in the Church (although I do not think you can assume that will always be the case), but a different sort of persistence has been necessary in the face of institutional inertia and marginalisation. In June last year the Anglican Mission in England was formed and I ordained three courageous young men from Southwark Diocese in the Kenyan bush, but this was a last resort after four years of discussion with senior Anglican leaders in England failed to find a way in which those genuinely in need of effective orthodox oversight in the Church of England could receive it.

This courage to persist can be tested by the temptation to despair. Physical courage is normally something of the moment – a particular threat that has to be faced at a particular moment – but the courage we are called to exercise is to commit ourselves to the long haul in a spiritual struggle which manifests itself not only in outward circumstances, but also within our own hearts.

I expect all of us know that there are times when we are tempted to lose heart. This temptation is subtle because it doesn't look like a temptation – we face discouragement and weariness to the extent that facts present themselves to us in such a way that it begins to look obvious that we should simply give up. Things seem to be beyond our capacities. But if so, we should be encouraged that even the Apostle Paul has been in that place. In 2 Corinthians 1:8,9 he says that he and his companions '*were under great pressure, far beyond our ability to endure, so that we despaired even of life. Indeed, in our hearts we felt the sentence of death. But this happened that we might not rely on ourselves but on God, who raises the dead.'*

The task God has given us for the reform and renewal of the Communion is a truly monumental task. The pressures in your context will be experienced in different ways from those in America or Africa, but it is the same spiritual battle and perhaps more is at stake here, especially in the Church of England as the historic mother church of the Communion. At times you may feel that you have completely exhausted your own abilities and energy, but praise the Lord that we know and trust in the God who does indeed raise the dead. If we will allow these experiences to throw us back on the all sufficient grace of God, then this Fellowship in which we share will be strong, an unstoppable force which will achieve all that awaits us in the Lord's purposes.

Finally, let us be very clear that although we stand firm, we are not reactionary. We are not trying to turn the clock back, nor do we have any desire to be judgemental as we speak in the name of the one who was the friend of sinners. What motivates our action is love. Let me remind you of how Paul finishes his list of exhortations in 1 Corinthians 16:14; he says **'do everything in love'**. We stand firm because we love the Lord Jesus Christ and we love one another as those who are fellow heirs with Christ. So in that love of God, we want to share with you, the Fellowship of Confessing Anglicans in the UK and Ireland, so that it may be clear to everyone that we are one in Christ, proclaiming the gospel fearlessly as we stand shoulder to shoulder and trust God for the fruit – and to be with us whatever the consequences. This love we have is not just the assent of our minds, but the passion of our hearts for the glory of God and the reconciliation of a lost humanity. Our Fellowship exists that we as Anglicans may bear clear and confident witness to the God who *'so loved the world that he gave his one and only Son, that whoever believes in him shall not perish but have eternal life. not perish'.* (John 3:16)

May the Lord strengthen you with all the riches of his grace and equip you for every good work as you trust in him. Amen

This address was given in London on Thursday 26ᵗʰ April 2012 at a separate meeting while Archbishop Wabukala was attending the Global FCA Leaders' Conference.

THE TRUTH SHALL SET YOU FREE

The Contributors

The Revd Canon Arthur Middleton

Canon Middleton read theology at King's College London and St Boniface College Warminster. He studied for a post-graduate research degree at Durham University and was awarded a Master of Letters. He is a Fellow of the Royal Historical Society and an Honorary Fellow of St. Chad's College Durham where he was Acting Principal and has served as a parish priest in Durham Diocese. His books include *Towards a Renewed Priesthood, Fathers and Anglican: The Limits of Orthodoxy, Prayer in the Workaday World,* and *Restoring the Anglican Mind* 1st &2nd editions published by Gracewing, *Ancient Words for a Present Grace* (Parish Press America).

The Right Revd Dr Michael Nazir-Ali

Bishop Michael Nazir-Ali was the 106th Bishop of Rochester until 2009. He was born in Pakistan and is a dual citizen of Pakistan and England. Bishop Nazir-Ali holds a BA from Karachi in Economics, Islamic History and Sociology, a B.Litt and an M.Litt from Oxford and an M.Litt from Cambriidge along with other qualifications. He received his ThD from the Australian College of Theology in 1983, was awarded a Lambeth DD in 2005 and holds numerous honorary degrees. He has taught in universities around the world and is an honorary fellow at both Oxford (St. Edmund Hall) and Cambridge (Fitzwilliam). Bishop Nazir-Ali is the author, most recently, of *Triple Jeopardy for the West: Aggressive Secularism, Radical Islamism and Multiculturalism* (Forthcoming, Continuum 2012), *The Unique and Universal Christ* (Paternoster, 2008), *Conviction and Conflict: Islam, Christianity and World Order* (Continuum, 2006) and a number of other books as well as numerous publications.

The Revd Professor Stephen Noll

Stephen Noll served as Vice Chancellor of Uganda Christian University from 2000-2010. He is Emeritus Professor at Trinity School for Ministry, where he taught for 21 years. He was a member of the statement committee at GAFCON 2008 and serves as a member of the GFCA Theological Commission. This essay is adapted from his essay, "Communion Governance: The Role and Future of the Episcopate and

the Anglican Communion Covenant" http://www.stephenswitness.org/
2012/02/communion-governance-role-and-future-of.html).

The Revd Dr Ashley Null

Ashley Null is an authority on the theology of Thomas Cranmer. He
received his PhD from Cambridge University and his MDiv as well as
his STM from Yale Divinity School. He is the author of *Thomas
Cranmer's Doctrine of Repentance: Renewing the Power to Love* (Oxford
2000) and is currently editing Cranmer's theological notebooks, a five-
volume series, for OUP as well. His research has received Fulbright,
Lighfoot, NEH and Guggenheim awards. He is the Canon Theologian
for the Diocese of Western Kansas as well as a fellow of two British
learned associations, the Society of Antiquaries and the Royal Historical
Society. A modified version of these lectures was published in Michael
P. Jensen, *Church of the Triune God: A tribute to Robert Doyle* (Sydney:
Aquila Press, 2013).

Dr Mrs Ngozi Okeke (Nneobioma)

Dr Mrs Ngozi Okeke began her theological training with the Sudan
Interior Mission in Nigeria where she obtained a BTh. After further
study at Wheaton College Illinois she moved to the UK with her
husband who was serving with the Church Mission Society as a reverse
missionary and gained her Masters and Ph. D degrees at King's College
London. In 2000, she went back to Nigeria when her husband was
appointed Bishop on the Niger, one of the oldest sees in the Church of
Nigeria. She is very passionate about making the Gospel the focus of
the Church's mission and ran seminars to equip the clergy and laity to
face effectively the challenges of living out the faith in the 21st Century.
She participated in the drafting of the Jerusalem Declaration and was a
member of the GAFCON Theological Resource Group. She and her
husband (now retired) currently organise training for the bishops of the
Church of Nigeria.

The Revd Dr Michael Ovey

Mike Ovey is Principal and Lecturer in Doctrine & Apologetics at Oak
Hill College, London. After a career as a civil service lawyer drafting
government legislation, he trained for the Church of England ordained
ministry at Ridley Hall, Cambridge, and worked as a curate for four
years at All Saints, Crowborough, before teaching for three years at
Moore Theological College, Sydney. He joined Oak Hill in 1998 and
since then has finished a PhD in the field of Trinitarian theology. In

addition to his college work he speaks more widely on the Cross and the doctrine of God and has co-authored a book on the substitutionary death of the Lord Jesus Christ.

The Revd Charles Raven

Charles Raven is Archbishop's Officer for Anglican Communion Affairs, Anglican Church of Kenya and serves as Secretary of the Global Fellowship of Confessing Anglicans Theological Commission. Previously he was Rector of Christ Church Wyre Forest, an Anglican Mission in England congregation in Worcestershire, England and before moving to Nairobi authored many articles and essays on the Anglican Communion. His book *Shadow Gospel: Rowan Williams and the Anglican Communion Crisis* was published by The Latimer Trust in 2010.

Dr Colin Reed

Colin Reed was born and grew up in Africa. He and his wife worked in Kenya and Tanzania for twenty years. Colin's Masters degree and Doctorate were on aspects of church history in East Africa, and he has written several books and articles on this topic, including 'Walking in the Light: Reflections on the East African Revival and its links to Australia'. Colin and his wife now live in Australia but he continues to visit East Africa.

The Revd Dr Mark Thompson

Mark Thompson is Principal of Moore Theological College, Sydney where he has been teaching doctrine since 1991. He also heads the Theology, Philosophy and Ethics Department. He is a member of the Sydney Synod and its Standing Committee and is Canon of St Andrews Cathedral Sydney. He is also the Chair of the Sydney Diocesan Doctrine Commission. He served on the GAFCON Theological Resource Group from 2008–2012 and now serves on the GFCA Theological Commission. He is the author of *A Clear and Present Word: The Clarity of Scripture* (2006) and joint editor of *The Gospel to the Nations* (2000), *Engaging Calvin* (2009), *The Faith Once For all Delivered* (2005) and *The Lord's Supper in Human Hands* (2008). He has written the article on 'GAFCON' in the Wiley-Blackwell *Companion to the Anglican Communion* (2013).

The Most Revd Dr Eliud Wabukala

Archbishop Wabukala is Archbishop of Kenya, Bishop of All Saints Cathedral Diocese, Nairobi and Chairman of the Global Fellowship of

Confessing Anglicans and its Primates Council. He received his PhD in New Testament studies at Wycliffe College, University of Toronto, in Canada, and he was subsequently appointed academic dean of St. Paul's Theological College in Limuru, Kenya. He was elected the first Bishop of Bungoma 1996 and was Chairman of the National Council of Churches of Kenya from 2005-2009, playing a key role in ending the outbreak of violence after the 2007 elections.

The Revd Dr John W Yates, III

John Yates III is Rector of Holy Trinity Anglican Church in Raleigh, N. Carolina. He received his PhD in New Testament studies from Cambridge University. Prior to that he completed a MA in Systematic Theology under Colin Gunton at King's College, London, and his M.Div. at Trinity School for Ministry, Ambridge. John is the author of *The Spirit and Creation in Paul* (Mohr-Siebeck, 2008), and has contributed to various edited volumes and periodicals.

If you have enjoyed this book, you might like to consider

- *supporting the work of the Latimer Trust*
- *reading more of our publications*
- *recommending them to others*

See www.latimertrust.org for more information.

LATIMER PUBLICATIONS

LATIMER STUDIES

LATIMER PUBLICATIONS

LATIMER BRIEFINGS

LATIMER PUBLICATIONS